# *Goren's*

## CANASTA
## UP-TO-DATE

# *Goren's*
# CANASTA
# UP - TO - DATE

*by*

## CHARLES H. GOREN

*Permabooks*

14 WEST 49TH STREET
NEW YORK, N.Y.

1950
PERMABOOKS

*Copyright, 1950, by Charles H. Goren*

## CONTENTS

# CONTENTS

# I

# The Elements of Canasta

## MECHANICS OF THE GAME

Canasta is a game of the rummy family. Its basic principles can, therefore, readily be grasped by anyone who has previously played any of the great number of rummy games that have been popular for several generations. And even those who have never been exposed to playing cards of any kind should not experience too much difficulty in acquainting themselves with the fundamentals, after which proficiency at the game may follow in short order.

The game in its most interesting form is designed for four players playing as two partnerships. However, it may also be played as a two-handed and three-handed game. And there are varieties of the game for five and six players. These will be discussed at greater length subsequently in this book. For the purposes of discussion it is to be presumed, where not otherwise indicated, that the game is being played by four characters, who for proper indentification will be referred to as North, East,

South, and West. (There may be other ways of painting the picture but it is not to be expected that this old dog, after his many years of addressing bridge audiences, should be taught new tricks of presentation.)

### THE DECK

The main item of equipment, the pack, consists of two full decks of playing cards to which are added four Jokers, making a complete contingent of 108 cards, shading by a narrow margin the deck used in the game of Oklahoma, but not even approaching the bulk of the equipment employed in Chinese (6 pack) Bezique.

Packs have been specially marketed for this game, which have the same colored backs, but this is by no means an essential feature. A Canasta deck may be composed by adding two packs of the conventional type and of different designs. This should present no difficulty because each new pack contains a standard Joker and an extra card that may be used as a Joker, so that the full complement of 108 cards is readily available.

In other card games the work of shuffling is usually assigned to the player at the left of the dealer.

In this game, it's maid's day out. Everybody should lend a hand in order to attain a better shuffle. I have never yet seen the player who could unassisted handle the 108 cards effectively. If you can do it, I feel confident that I can find a spot for you on Arthur Godfrey's talent show.

### WILD CARDS

The Jokers are "wild" cards; that is to say, they may be named as any card their possessor chooses, from the 4 to the Ace.[1] The Joker or deuce may be named as a Black Three at the time of going out, but this will be taken up at a later time.

The deuces are also wild cards, so that there are in all, 12 wild cards, which should be sufficient to whet even the most jaded appetite.

### POINTS OF SIMILARITY TO OTHER RUMMY GAMES

As in all games of the rummy family play ceases when one of the players "goes out." That is to say, when a player (in legal manner) disposes of all of

---

[1] In counting up the cards for the purpose of computing the score, the Joker counts 50 points and the deuce 20 points, regardless of what cards they represent.

his cards. In the process of going out, the object of the game is the accumulation of as many points as possible. These points are scored by earning various bonuses and spreading various melds, which will presently be discussed.

The game has the following features in common with other rummy games: *The Stock* (more properly referred to as the stock pile): This is the remainder of the deck that is left after each player has been dealt the number of cards assigned to him by the rules; in other words, the undealt portion of the deck. It is from this PILE that the players in their proper turn draw their cards one at a time during the course of play.

*The Discard Pile:* In all rummy games after drawing and completing a play, a player is required to make a discard. These discards are accumulated in a pile, which in Canasta soon becomes the cynosure of all eyes.

*The Meld:* Melding or spreading is common to all rummy games. As in all games of this family, the meld is an optional procedure. The possessor of a "spread" is not required to meld it. He does so at his own discretion.

*The Pay-off:* In all rummy games a player receives credit for the value of the cards which have made up his exposed melds, whereas he must pay for those cards which he retains in his hand, when play has ceased.[2]

*The Suits Have No Significance:* In most rummy games, a sequence of at least three cards in the same suit is a meld, frequently called a "spread" or "run." Thus the 7-8-9 of Hearts, or the K-Q-J of Spades are eligible to be melded. But in Canasta the sequence is not recognized. And since there is no distinction as to suits the only melds are "three of a kind" or more. In this respect it is similar to poker. You may meld three Aces (or more), three Jacks, three fours, etc.

*No Lay-off on Opponent's Meld:* In many games of the rummy family, a player is permitted to play cards which may be added to the melds of an opponent. In gin rummy one "lays off" on the adversary's meld. This is also true in Persian rummy. But this is not permitted in Canasta. You may add addi-

---

[2]This does not, however, hold true in the game of gin rummy, where a player may meld any spreads his hand contains, when his opponent goes down by knocking.

tional cards only to the melds that have been made by your side.

*Taking the Discard:* In games like gin rummy, if your opponent has been charitable enough to part with a card which you find to your taste, you reach gently though firmly for that particular card and add it to your hand, ignoring the rest of the discard pile. But in Canasta (just as in the game of Oklahoma) if you wish the top card, the whole discard pile goes with it. You take the mother-in-law along with the bride. You will find it however, more acceptable in this case, than in the field of marital relations. Far from being a burden, you will find it highly advantageous to become the possessor of a great quantity of cards. But this feature of the game will be discussed under the heading of tactics.

*Restriction on Use of Wild Cards:* Unlike other games in which the use of wild cards is unrestricted, the employment of the Jokers and deuces in Canasta is confined within specified limits. In the game of Oklahoma for example, a player may spread three deuces and call them three Aces. Or he may spread three deuces and the Queen of Hearts, and call the meld Ace, King, Queen, Jack of Hearts. This is not permitted in the game of Canasta. *Each*

*meld must contain at least two natural cards, and
no meld may contain more than three wild cards,
except as provided in law 33.* It will be observed
presently that some melds run as high as seven or
more cards (A Canasta is a meld of 7 of a kind)
but at least four of them must be natural cards.

### THE RED THREE

The red three has a special status in the game.
It is a mere bonus card and never takes part in the
actual play of the hand. The position of the red
trey is somewhat like "honors" in bridge. The bonus
(100 points) is awarded to the side that has them,
merely for possession. The fact that honors are held,
has no bearing on the actual play of the cards.

If the first turned card is a red three it may not
be picked up. It is covered by the next card from
the up-pile and play proceeds in the normal manner. The red three as well as all the other cards that
have been discarded on top of it, will eventually
become the possession of the player who is fortunate
enough to be able to pick up the discard pile. But
the red three never becomes part of anyone's hand.
It must be placed upon the table immediately at

the beginning of play. If one is dealt to a player, he waits until his first turn to play, places it on the table, draws from the stock to replenish his hand, and then makes his play. If a player has two or more red threes he draws the same number of cards from the stock to bring his hand up to the required number of cards before proceeding with his play.

If during the progress of the game a player draws a red three from the stock, he is required to face it upon the table immediately and draw another card to replace it.

If a player has picked up a red three in the discard pile (it could have gotten there only by being turned up at the beginning of play) he must face it upon the table, but in this case he does not draw a card from the stock to replace it.

The bonus for each red three is 100 points, but the bonus is doubled if one side happens to collect all four red threes. While the bonus collected for possession of the red threes may come as a highly acceptable windfall there is nevertheless at times a darker side to the picture, for there is a hardship attached to the ownership of these "flowers" where the side possessing them has not made a meld at the time that their opponents go out on that particular hand. In such unfortunate cases, the side is charged with 100 points for each red three as the price for being "caught" with them. And if a side has faced all 4 red threes and has not succeeded in making a meld when that hand is over (a gruesome state of affairs) 800 points are deducted from their score.

### THE BLACK THREE

The black three has a special status in the game. During the course of the play a meld of any number of threes is not permitted. They may be melded at the end of the hand, as a player is "going out", at which time three or four of them may be spread. In the original code propounded in the Argentine, the final meld of threes must include only natural cards, that is to say, a player was not permitted to meld two black threes and a wild card. But in the rules as modified by the Regency Club of New York, the deuce or Joker may be added to a pair of black threes to complete a meld which permits that player to go out.

It would therefore seem, at first glance, that the black three would play a very subordinate role in the show. Actually the contrary is true, because that card is invested with a special authority. It may not be picked up by the next player. In other words, when a black three is discarded, the next player must draw from the stock pile. The strategic use of this card will be discussed in a later chapter of this book.

### FREEZING THE PACK
(*Making a prize pile*)

A unique feature of the game is the practice known as freezing the pack, or as the Argentines refer to it "making a prize pile." While normally a player may take up the discard pile if he can match the last discard, with one other of the kind and a wild card (making three of a kind and therefore a legal meld), when the pack is frozen a wild card may not be used for the purpose of taking up the discard pile. A player in order to be qualified to take up the pile must then produce a natural pair to match the card last thrown by his adversary. The pack may be deliberately frozen by the discard of a wild card and many times it is good strategy to do so, even at the expense of giving up your only wild card. But this will be discussed more fully in the chapter on tactics.

## THE CANASTA

The Canasta, from which the game takes its name, is a meld of 7 or more of a kind. This may be made up of all natural cards, in which case one is said to have a pure or natural Canasta. A mixed Canasta may include any number of wild cards provided it includes at least four natural cards. A side cannot go out without first having completed a Canasta. Completion of a Canasta therefore is the essential goal. Unless one scores in this fashion he cannot win.

The preceding chapter represents briefly the salient distinguishing characteristics of the game of Canasta. There are others of lesser significance, but they will be pointed out in proper sequence as the mechanics of the game are uncovered. It was our purpose in the section above to give you a short preview of the game as a whole, before proceeding with a blow by blow description of a typical fracas.

## THE PRELIMINARIES

Partnerships are determined in the conventional manner by the drawing of cards. The players drawing the two high cards become partners against the other two. This ceremony is dispensed with, of course, where a challenge match has previously been arranged (an occurrence which not uncommonly results after a heated discussion between players and the usual outburst "Get yourself a partner"!). But in that case the cards are cut to determine the dealer.

The deal does not go to the player cutting the high card, as in bridge. In bridge the deal is sought after, for dealer has the first bid which confers upon him a distinct advantage. In Canasta there is a slight advantage in making the first play, so the winner of the cut (high card) is dealt to, inasmuch as the player to the dealer's left makes the first play.

In cutting, Jokers do not count. A player, drawing a Joker, sets it aside and draws another card. For purposes of the cut, the Ace is high and the deuce is low, and if players draw cards of the same size, the tie is broken on the basis of suit superiority, and the suits for this purpose rank as in bridge, that is, Spades are highest, then Hearts, Diamonds and Clubs, in that order.

This is the only time cognizance is taken of the suits. Remember that in the play of the game of Canasta, it is as though suits did not exist (except for the purpose of distinguishing between black threes and red threes).

The dealer of the first hand is determined by the cut. Thereafter the deal rotates in a clockwise direction (to the left, if you will pardon my being so specific). I know one player who remembers the rotation of the deal by recalling that it goes in the opposite direction from race horses (readers in Great Britain will please ignore). Before the deal, any player who is eager beaver enough to wish to shuffle has the right to do so.

Before distributing the cards, dealer gives them to the player on his right to cut. In order to be legal a cut must contain at least four cards. The cards are distributed one at a time in the conventional clockwise manner until each player has eleven. (Remember we are discussing the four handed version of the game. In three handed, each player receives thirteen cards, and in the two handed game each player is dealt fifteen cards.) The remainder of the pack, which has not been dealt is then placed down, presumably within easy reach of all the contestants, and becomes known as the stock pile. A card is then turned face up on table, and is known as the "up-card."

The next step is the extraction of the red threes

dealt the first player. Before making his play, if holding one or more red threes he faces them on the table and takes from the stock pile as many cards as he faced red threes; in other words he must restore his hand to eleven cards. The other players go through the same procedure when their respective turns to play arrive.

After each player has received his 11 cards, the next card is turned and is referred to as the "up card". This is the beginning of what is known as the "discard pile" or "up pile". All subsequent discards are placed face upward in a pile, on that card. That is, of course, presuming that the first player does not take it up, which is his prerogative if he can meet the prescribed requirements.

Let us, for purposes of illustration, examine an imaginary deal: South has cut the highest card. North, the next highest (that is how they became partners). South has the privilege of playing first, so East deals. The second hand, if all the players survive the ordeal, will be dealt by South, and if there is a third hand before the game has been won, West will be the dealer, and so on.

Eleven cards have been dealt to each of the players and a card turned face up—"the up card". The balance of the cards (the stock pile) has been placed face down in the center of the table. East, the dealer, turns to South who appears to be in a bit of a fog, and to speed up matters inquires, "Have you any red threes?" South decides he has none, and makes his regular play, whereupon it is up to West, who quickly faces a red three on the table in front of him (and it is well that he keep it there, for it carries a bonus of 100 points). He reaches into the stock pile for another card to restore his hand to eleven, completes his maneuver, and play proceeds to North. North too, faces a red three and because his part of the table is crowded with an ash tray and a drink, he appoints South, his partner, custodian of the loot and places the red three in front of him. It is customary for one partner to collect the meld while the other keeps score. But North is sure to get the score pad all wet so South has agreed to do both. North then reaches into the stock pile to replenish his hand, and comes up like Little Jack Horner with a "What a good boy am I!" another red three! He places it beside the other one in front of South and tries again. This time he evidently drew a more normal card, his hand now contains the conventional eleven cards and play proceeds to East. East denies possession of a red three. He had better be right for if at the conclusion of the hand it is discovered that he failed to put down a red three he is subject to a penalty of 500 points. I have seldom seen this penalty incurred and little wonder; forgetting to expose a red three is about on a par with losing a bass drum.

The up-card chanced to be the 7 of Spades. The suit has no significance as far as play is concerned; it is merely a 7, and its complexion does not concern us.

We gaze into South's hand and find that he was dealt the following:

K-K-Q-J    9-8-7-6-6    3-2

You will observe that he has no use for the 7. He has a 7 and a deuce in his hand and using the wild deuce as a 7 he could claim a meld of three 7s, but there are two reasons why he may not do so, which we will point out in a moment, so he reaches into the stock pile for his first draw. Note that the 7 was available only to South and not to any other player at the table. In this respect Canasta differs from Gin or Oklahoma, where the player, who has been dealt to, has the choice of taking the up-card but if he declines it, the option to take it up passes to the next player. South draws an 8. Having made his DRAW it becomes South's turn to MELD, if he chooses, and if he is legally able to. In order to be able to comply with the legal requirements for making the first meld, South would have to be able to show at least three of a kind, with a count of at least 50 points. South could spread the pair of 9s with the deuce (which is a wild card and may be named as a 9). This would give him three of a kind but the count would reach only 40 (20 for the deuce and 10 for each of the 9s). He is, therefore, not in a position to make his initial meld. Later in the game after he or his partner has made an initial meld, subsequent melds of any three cards, even if they total only 15 points, will be permitted. Having *drawn* and passed the opportunity to *meld*, South *must* now make a DISCARD. South chooses to discard the 8, for which he has no use. He might perhaps have discarded the 7, which is a low card (counts only 5 points: the high cards K-Q-J-10-9-8 count 10 points each).

There is an exception to the rule that your first meld must contain at least 50 points. If on the first hand your side has "gone in the hole", that is, you made a minus score, then there is no restriction as to your first meld on the following hand. You may make it with as little as 15 points, that is a spread of three low cards.

But as play progresses and your score mounts, there are stricter requirements for making the first meld.

If your score is between 1500 and 2995 your first meld must consist of at least 90 points. And when your score is 3000 or more, you may not make the initial meld for your side unless you can spread 120 points, though you may do so in one set, two sets or three sets.

It's weight for age, so to speak. The younger horses are required to carry less weight than the older ones.

Now that South has concluded his play by discarding, the scene progresses to West.

Mounting our trusty revolving stage we peer into his hand and find:

Joker-A-K-Q-8-5-5-5-4-4-2

You might suggest that West take up the 8, match it with his own 8 and the deuce, melding three 8s for a count of 40 points together with his three 5s, making 55 points in all, but this may not be done. Later in the hand such action will be permissible but in the early part of the hand a team that has not yet made its first meld, is not permitted to take up the discard pile with the aid of a wild card. The player who wishes to take the "up pile" must show a natural pair to match the top card of the pile (the most recent discard). West, therefore, makes his DRAW from the stock pile. He draws a 6. It is his privilege to MELD if he can produce a 50 point spread. For this purpose he may use a wild card. He, therefore, spreads:

Joker-4-4 (60 points—50 for the Joker and 5 each for the low cards).

He could also spread in addition:

$$5\text{-}5\text{-}5$$

if he chose, but he need not; and he decides to hold back for a while. He discards the 6, which he has just drawn.

It is North's turn to play. His hand consists of

$$A\text{-}K\text{-}J\text{-}J\text{-}10\text{-}9\text{-}5\text{-}5\text{-}4\text{-}4\text{-}2$$

Unable to use the up card, he draws from the stock, and plucks a King. He discards the 9.

East holds

$$A\text{-}Q\text{-}10\text{-}10\text{-}10\text{-}9\text{-}9\text{-}7\text{-}4\text{-}4\text{-}2$$

Having a natural pair to match the top of the discard pile, it is his prerogative to take up the pile.

Proper procedure is to establish his right to take it by just exposing his pair of 9s.

Note that his meld counts only 30 points, but since his partner has already made an initial meld for his side, he is not subject to the 50 point rule and may go in for any three card meld. Notice, too, that East could have gone in for the 9 if he chose even if he had held only one of them, for he could have used the deuce in place of a 9. (That is because his side had already made its initial meld—prior to that time one must produce a natural pair to be entitled to go in.)

East then places the three 9s in front of his partner, who, you will recall, has previously melded Joker-4-4 and has been designated as the official depository for the team of East and West. East also picks up the other two cards which have been discarded by South and West, plus the original up card. At this time East is privileged to meld anything else he chooses, but he is under no obligation to do so. East actually adds two 4s to his partner's meld, holds up his three 10s and discards the 8 which he has picked up in the stack and which South originally discarded.

This completes the first round and play progresses in that order.

Play continues until one side has been able to meld its entire hand (or all but one card which may be discarded). But before a side may meld out it must first have completed a Canasta (7 of a kind). The bonus for going out is only 100 points. Or the deal may end when the stock pile is exhausted and no one is able to make any further plays, in this case there is no "going out" bonus.

At the conclusion of each hand players are charged for all cards remaining in their hands for which a deduction is made from the credits for melds and bonuses. The principal bonuses are those awarded for completed Canastas—500 points for a natural Canasta—containing no wild cards, and 300 points for any Canasta that contains one or more wild cards. The mixed Canasta must contain at least four natural cards.

After a Canasta has been completed a team may add cards of the same rank to it. For example— you have completed a Canasta of seven Jacks, four natural Jacks and three wild cards; later if you draw a Jack you may add it to your Canasta. The bonus for this Canasta still remains at 300 points. All you have done is added 10 points in card value to your hand. This process may be repeated if you draw another Jack. It will be shown later on that the melding of this extra Jack is not good strategy, unless it permits you to go out by clearing your hand.

The addition of a wild card may be made to a completed Canasta. You may even add a wild card to a natural Canasta, but then the Canasta loses its natural quality and becomes a mixed Canasta. This is a rare occurrence and could come about in some such manner as this:—your side has completed, let us say, three natural Canastas and no other melds, you are down to two cards, a deuce and an odd card. It is your desire to go out. You could meld the deuce on one of your Canastas and discard the odd card. If you had any other meld, you would naturally add the deuce to such meld, and not disturb the purity of your Canastas.

During the course of play, if your right hand opponent discards a card which matches one of your exposed melds you have the right to take it up, and with it the entire discard pile, adding the up card to your meld. Such a card is commonly referred to as a "player" because it can be "played" on one of your melds.

The latter provision does not apply when the discard pile is "frozen." When the up pile contains a wild card or a red 3 it is said to be frozen. It is then more difficult to take it up. (A red 3 can only get in there by being turned as the original up card, a wild card may also get there in that manner.) When the discard pile has not been originally frozen by the accident of the up card, it may be frozen deliberately by any player discarding a deuce or a Joker.

When the discard pile is frozen it may be taken up only by a player who can produce a *natural pair* to match the current up card. An ordinary "player" (that is a card that matches one of your exposed melds) may not be picked up during the "freeze" unless the next player happens to have a concealed natural pair to match that discard.

When a frozen pile is taken up, that is the end of the freeze and play starts over in a natural manner, until someone else chooses to freeze it again by discarding a wild card.

# II

## Glossary of Canasta Terms

A Canasta is a set of seven cards of a kind without regard to the suits. That is to say, 7 Jacks or 7 Fives make a Canasta.

There are two types of Canasta, the pure or natural, and the mixed. A pure Canasta consists of 7 cards of the same rank without any wild cards. The following are natural or pure Canastas:

$$Q\text{-}Q\text{-}Q\text{-}Q\text{-}Q\text{-}Q\text{-}Q$$
$$6\text{-}6\text{-}6\text{-}6\text{-}6\text{-}6\text{-}6$$

A mixed Canasta consists of a set of 7 cards of which some are wild cards. A mixed Canasta must contain at least four natural cards. This will permit three wild cards. If there are five natural cards you will need but two wild cards, and if there are six natural cards only one wild card will be needed to complete the Canasta. Additional cards, either wild or natural, may be added to any Canasta. The following are examples of mixed Canastas:

$$2\text{-}Q\text{-}Q\text{-}Q\text{-}Q\text{-}Q\text{-}Q$$
$$2\text{-}2\text{-}2\text{-}9\text{-}9\text{-}9\text{-}9$$
$$Joker\text{-}2\text{-}7\text{-}7\text{-}7\text{-}7\text{-}7$$

The following, however, is not a legal Canasta because it contains too many wild cards, or to put it another way, not enough natural cards:

$$Joker\text{-}2\text{-}2\text{-}2\text{-}Q\text{-}Q\text{-}Q$$

For purposes of distinguishing between a pure Canasta and a mixed Canasta after they have been completed and stacked together, it is customary to identify them by the top card. After folding a Canasta, if it is a pure one, it is the practice to place a red card face upward on the top. If it is a mixed Canasta, it is the custom to place a black natural card on top of the seven card stack.

### MELD

A meld is a set of three or more cards of the same rank. It must always contain at least two natural cards. That is to say, it may consist of three natural cards or two natural cards and a wild one. The following are legal melds:

$$9\text{-}9\text{-}9$$
$$9\text{-}9\text{-}2$$

The following is not a legal meld:

2-2-9

Melds that have been exposed on the table count in favor of the side that has exposed them. But those that remain in the hand of the player are scored against him at the conclusion of the hand.

### UP-PILE

This is also referred to as the discard pile. Each player in turn makes a draw and a discard. The up-pile is the collection of these discards, and it is maintained by placing one card on top of the other so that only the most recent discard is exposed to view. The top card of the discard pile, in other words, the most recent discard, is frequently referred to as the "up-card."

### UP-CARD

The up-card is the top card of the discard pile. It may be the only one in the pile, as when the discard pile is started by the dealer. It is then the original up card. It may also be the only one in the pile, when a player goes in for the discard pile, melds and makes a discard. That discard becomes the up-card and until the next discard is the only card in the pile.

### HIGH CARD

The term "high-card" is loosely used to refer to any card of the value of 10 points to distinguish it from the lower cards, that is

$$K\text{-}Q\text{-}J\text{-}10\text{-}9\text{-}8$$

The Ace is, for this purpose, in a category of its own for its value is 20 points.

### LOW CARD

The term "low-card" refers to cards of the value of 5 points namely

$$7\text{-}6\text{-}5\text{-}4\text{-}\text{black threes}$$

### PRIZE PILE

Otherwise known as a frozen pack. The discard pile becomes a prize pile (that is, it is frozen) when one of the players discards a Joker or a deuce into the discard pile. The up-pile also becomes frozen if the dealer exposes a Joker, a deuce or a red trey on the first upturned card.

When the discard pile is frozen, any player may continue to discard wild cards, but that has no additional effect upon the freeze. There are no degrees of "frost". The discard pile is either frozen or it is not, and it does not matter after a pile has been frozen that further wild cards have been thrown into it.

### STOP CARD

The black trey is known as a stop card. When it is the most recent discard the next player is not permitted to go into the discard pile but must draw from the stack. But the presence of the black three in the pile has no further effect after the next player draws and discards. In other words, it is a one-play stop card.

### THE RED TREY

The red three has a special status. It does not take part in the actual play of a hand. It is a mere bonus card and must be exposed by the player immediately, whether he receives it on the deal or draws it during the course of play. As it is exposed, a replacement card is drawn from the stock pile. The red three carries a bonus of 100 points though it does not figure in the play of the hand. It's more in the nature of a door prize. If one side obtains all four red threes the bonus is 800 points.

If a hand ends before a side has made its first meld, its red treys are counted against the possessor instead of for him, that is, the bonus is deducted.

Red threes taken in a prize pile are exposed but not replaced by a draw from the stock pile.

### A CONCEALED HAND

This is the case in which a player melds his entire hand at once, without having previously melded. There is a special bonus of 100 points for melding out with a concealed hand, provided the player does not meld any of his cards, on his partner's meld.

### ASKING PERMISSION

A novel feature of the game of Canasta, is this limited consultation between partners. When a player contemplates going out, after drawing but before playing, he is permitted to ask his partner "Shall I go out?" The partner answers "Yes" or "No" and the person inquiring is bound by the answer. A player may go out without asking partner's permission.

# III

# The Higher Strategy

It is not a simple matter to clarify the strategy of Canasta. The number of possible combinations is so great that we cannot hope to do any more than hand out broad general principles for the student to follow. The strategy of the game divides itself into various fields of action. Treating the various subjects in their logical order, we take up first the question of

## THE INITIAL MELD

Where it is convenient to do so, the initial meld should be made as early in the hand as possible, for the team which melds first has a decided advantage over its opponents. It has been pointed out that until a team has made its initial meld, discard pile so far as that team is concerned remains frozen. In other words, the pile may be taken up only with a natural pair which matches the up card. At such time a player is not in a position to take advantage of the "wild" features of the Jokers and deuces. But after you have made the initial meld your side may take the discard pile with the aid of a wild card and only one card matching the top of the discard pile.

Making the initial meld also has the effect of taking the burden off your partner's shoulders. He may have been straining to make the initial meld and your doing so will have put an end to his problem.

However, making the initial meld frequently involves a sacrifice, the sacrifice of giving up an important part of your hand. When that is the case, a player must weigh carefully the advantages and disadvantages of making the initial meld. At the early stages of the game, when only 50 points are required, one should not hasten to spread the first meld if such action will require the use of a great number of cards. We cannot stress too violently the dangers of depleting your hand early in the game. Cards are your ammunition. If the enemy have a great many more than you, you are in serious danger of being annihilated. It may therefore be laid down as a rule that if the initial meld will require as many as six of your cards, the action should be postponed for a round or two. A short delay may bring about an improvement in conditions. You may then be able to take up the discard pile as you make your initial

meld. When this can be done very little consideration is given to the number of cards needed from
your hand for the purpose. The reason is obvious—
your hand will be replenished to a certain extent by
the cards you take up from the discard pile.

To spread six cards early in the play leaves you
with only six, which is extremely ineffective ammunition. When your hand is reduced to but six cards
your prospects of building future melds are not very
bright, remember it is melds, which are the back-
bone of winning Canasta. Unlike the game of Oklahoma, one gives scant consideration to the act of
going out, for the going out bonus is relatively insig-
nificant, and the act of going out should be inci-
dental to the main object and strategy of the game.
Never lose sight of the principle that you cannot
hope to score heavily without a great many cards.
Keep collecting them. Whether or not to hurry the
making of the initial meld will depend frequently on
whether the discard pile is frozen. Where it is frozen,
in many cases the advantage of making the initial
meld is considerably lessened, for your side will still
need a natural pair to go in. Then too, when the pile
is frozen a meld by your side may, to a certain extent, diminish your chances of taking the discard
pile, for your righthand opponent is in a position

where he can discard several cards of the same denomination as those which you have just melded. But if you can meld without using up too many cards and still retain several pairs with which to take up the discard pile later on, it is good practice to go down forthwith, especially if you have some reasonably safe discards available.

The ideal initial meld, when only 50 points are required, is three Aces. This uses up the least number of cards, which, incidentally, is the prime consideration in making the first meld. Furthermore, it does not require your giving up a wild card, which is the next important consideration. The retention of wild cards becomes important as the fight for the discard pile begins. When a player is fortunate enough to hold three Aces, he should meld them at once under all conditions. Next, from the standpoint of attractiveness as an initial meld, are a pair of Aces and a wild card. This is especially true if it is not your only wild card, so that you will still retain one in your hand to give comfort to you in your declining days.

After that, the next most desirable initial meld is a run of five high cards (each counting 10 points). If it will take four high cards and a deuce, it is a very close question whether to go down. If you have a deuce to spare, it is recommended that you make the

initial meld, but if that deuce is your only wild card
it is better to wait.

Some players make it a rule never to make an
initial meld of 50 out of their own hand, if it takes
more than 3 cards.

You need 50 for your initial meld and after drawing hold:—

2-A-Q-J-9-8-8-8-8-6-5-4

Would you make your initial meld?

You could do so by melding the deuce with your
8s, but our advice is strongly against it. You should
wait at least several draws. You may then be lucky
enough to have acquired the cards to permit a more
economical meld. If you go down at once you will be
left, after discarding, with this wretched holding:—

A-Q-J-9-6-5

a completely hopeless array of cards and in the absence of the most sensational draws by you and yeo-
man service by your partner, the rest of the deal will
be a completely boring affair.

If you wait a while before making your first meld
you may be lucky enough to draw a deuce, in which
case you may spread the 8s with one deuce and retain the other to help you get the discard pile, and

get back into business, or you may draw an Ace in which case you could meld much more economically by spreading 2-A-A.

If, after about four draws, you find that your hand has not improved because you have drawn a variety of cards which did not make up pairs in your hand, you may then decide to sacrifice yourself by going down with the deuce, and the 8s in the hope that partner will be able to carry on after you make the initial meld for your side.

Let us change the above hand slightly so that it consists of:—

$$2\text{-}A\text{-}Q\text{-}J\text{-}9\text{-}8\text{-}8\text{-}8\text{-}6\text{-}6\text{-}5\text{-}4$$

Here too, you need 50 points for the initial meld, and our advice again is not to go down. Though in this particular case we would not wait quite so long as in the case immediately preceding. We would be inclined to go down one round sooner, especially if we are lucky enough to draw a 4 or a 5 which with the 6s would give us two pairs and therefore an increased chance to get the pack.

On the subject of the economy of the initial meld, put it down as a rule that you *NEVER meld six cards if you are able to make the grade with only four cards.*

For example: Needing 50 you hold

2-Q-J-10-10-9-9-9-8-7-5-4

You could, if making your initial meld, select 2-10-10 and 9-9-9 consuming six cards in the process. This would be a highly unsound play. The initial meld can be made by spreading 2-9-9-9 using only four cards. Some players have advanced the argument that the former meld, though it uses six cards, has an advantage in that it starts toward two possible Canastas. This argument is fallacious and we beseech you to disregard it.

Even when your side needs 120 for the initial meld and it is therefore most urgent to go down, a delay of a round or two may be good strategy, if the initial meld will otherwise take your entire supply of Jokers.

For example: Both sides need 120; after drawing you hold

Joker-Joker-A-10-10-10-9-8-8-7-6-5

You could go down by melding Jokers and 10s or 8s, but it would be good speculation to wait at least a couple of rounds. Possession of two Jokers places you in a highly strategic position, the chances of the opposition being able to go down at 120 is considerably lessened by the likelihood that they haven't the necessary Jokers. So they are not to be feared. It is to your interest to see the pack grow heavy; you might even let go a 10, and perhaps acquire more pairs, so that eventually your right hand opponent will be squeezed into letting go a card of which you have a pair. The acquisition of the rich pile will then insure your scoring a big hand. With only one Joker, however, your advantage is not pronounced and you should not wait—go down as soon as you can.

Wild cards should be handled frugally during the early part of the game. If you have only two of them it is not sound practice to employ them both with a pair in order to make the initial meld, but if you are fortunate enough to have three wild cards, then there is no objection to melding two of them with a pair, since you will still retain one as an aid in obtaining the discard pile. In other words, giving up your only deuce is a highly undesirable procedure, and is frequently too great a price to pay for making the initial meld. It is highly desirable to meld Aces early in the game. The Ace (counting 20 points) is higher valued than any other natural card, and is therefore a great comfort to a player when he is seeking to make his count for the initial meld. It is for this reason that one should be wary of discarding Aces early in the game. When a player has one, he normally holds on to it in the hope of drawing one or two more in order to be able to meld them. It behooves either partner, therefore, to meld Aces promptly to provide the other with a parking place for Aces that show up as the hand develops. Assume that the game has just started, and you therefore need 50 points for your initial meld. After drawing you hold the following hand:

$$2\text{-}7\text{-}7\text{-}7\text{-}7\text{-}Q\text{-}Q\text{-}Q\text{-}K\text{-}9\text{-}5\text{-}4$$

You are in a position to make up the required count by melding Queens and sevens (50 points) but this would be suicidal play. You should delay going down for several rounds, for the offering up of seven cards for the purpose of the initial meld is out of the question.

You could, if you choose, meld your deuce with the three Queens. This takes only four cards and in that respect is not objectionable. But it involves giving up your only wild card, which except in extreme cases should be avoided. If you came down to a choice between going down with your seven natural cards and using your one deuce to meld with four cards, the latter would be a clear-cut choice. With this hand you may profit by a slight delay. If you draw a deuce you should certainly meld the three Queens, for you will still retain a deuce in your hand for emergencies. With the hand above, the wisest procedure would be to discard a seven. This does not damage your hand to any extent and may lure your right-hand opponent into discarding a seven if he has one; but this strategy will be discussed subsequently under the heading of deception.

It has been pointed out that when one needs 50 points only, the initial meld should be made at once if no more than 3 or 4 cards are needed for the purpose. When 90 points are required for the initial meld, it is somewhat more difficult to make the grade, and one must be prepared to invest six cards for that purpose, and sometimes even seven. But when it will take that many cards, it is better to wait a round or two in the hope that the next draw will effect an improvement in your hand. Where eight cards are required to make the initial meld, such a step should be delayed for a considerable time; and if it would require as many as nine, just be stubborn. Don't give up the ship.

Where your score is in the upper brackets and you consequently need 120 points for your initial meld, you are frequently up against a difficult task. The

importance of getting down becomes even more pronounced. A player can ill afford to be as fussy as he
was in the earlier stages of the game when only 50 or
90 were needed. Even if it should take six cards a
player ought to go down immediately at this score.
If it takes seven or eight, a little delay should be
tolerated. Sometimes it is necessary to ruin your
hand by melding nine cards when it seems that partner is unable to make the grade, and the chances of
improving your hand do not appear to be good.

When you have given up nine cards you will have,
in effect, eliminated yourself as a potent factor in the
game, and it will then be up to partner to carry the
ball from here in. But there is this thought to comfort you, that if partner is successful in obtaining the
up-pile, and as a consequence completes a Canasta,
you will be in a position to play for out, if any enemy
pressure begins to be felt.

We have been discussing the undesirability of giving up a great many cards for the purpose of making
the initial meld, but when in making your initial
meld, you can take the discard pile, you should do so
at almost any cost, especially if you are able to take
up a discard pile containing at least five or six cards.
As you make your initial meld you may have a
choice as to the manner in which to spread it. That

is to say, you may have several different pairs. It is good policy in such cases to meld those cards to which your partner will more likely be able to contribute. For example: Your side needs 90 for the initial meld, and after drawing your hand consists of

2-A-A-A-J-J-8-8-7-6-5-4

You will naturally spread the three Aces, and now you may meld (with your deuce) the pair of Jacks or the pair of eights. They both count the same. If you feel that your partner very likely has Jacks, that would be the pair to spread. On the other hand, if you thought there was a better chance that he held eights, you would, of course, meld that pair. In many cases you will be called upon to make an out-and-out guess. You may increase your chances of guessing correctly if you have been observing your partner's previous discards. If he has already thrown an eight, it is natural for you to assume that he is not saving eights, and that there is therefore a better chance that he will have one or more Jacks in his hand. In that case, your proper procedure is to meld your deuce with a pair of Jacks.

Where your side has a great many more cards than the opposition, you are safe to presume that you have control. At such times it may be good strategy to hold up your meld and keep your righthand opponent guessing as to what your hand contains. This will make his discarding problems more acute. When you have been able to take the discard pile to make your initial meld you will frequently find that you are in a position to make numerous other melds. There is usually no hurry about doing so. True enough, the more you meld the easier it is for your partner to get to work on the process of completing Canastas, but there is a certain advantage in holding up a great part of your meld. This will frequently be bewildering to your righthand opponent, who more likely than not, will be tricked into throwing cards which find matches in your hand, and which you find permit you to take the discard pile again.

Illustration: You need 50 for your initial meld, and after drawing you hold:

Joker-2-A-A-Q-J-8-8-7-6-6-4

You should meld Joker, Ace, Ace immediately. It will be observed that you could meld 2-A-A which would also meet the required count, but that would not be proper tactics. The Joker should always be melded in preference to the deuce. It counts 50 instead of 20, and furthermore, if you happen to be caught with the Joker it is at the cost of 50 points as against only 20 for the deuce. Whereas in the play of the hand the deuce has all the power of the Joker; so you might as well gain the greater score and at the same time run the less risk of loss. If with that same hand you needed 120, you could meet the requirements by melding the Joker with a pair of Aces, and the deuce with a pair of eights. But there is some question as to the advisability of such play. This method would have exhausted your entire supply of wild cards, a situation which should be avoided wherever possible. It might even be better strategy to wait for a round or two in the hope of drawing an eight so that you could make the initial meld and still retain your wild card.

### DISCARDING

Of paramount importance in the strategy of Canasta is the technique of proper discarding. If it were possible to condense the practice of sound discarding into a phrase, it would read something like this: "Keep your eye sharply fixed on your left-hand opponent. Watch carefully his discards for you are trying to discover what he wants and what he doesn't want".

Feed him on a diet of cards that you are con-

vinced he doesn't want. It is good practice to assume
that he has no use for the cards that he has been discarding. Mind you, this bit of advice is not offered
with any guarantee. You must expect to be the vic-
tim of deception now and then, for a crafty opponent will occasionally take you in by discarding some
cards that he actually wants. This cannot be helped.
After you have played any length of time with certain players you will familiarize yourself with some
of their traits, and perhaps your sixth sense will help
you to judge whether he is leading you on or whether
he is on the level.

In the long run, however, you will find it preferable to play the percentages and throw him the cards
that he has been tossing. In judging the cards your
lefthand opponent needs, you should be influenced
to a greater degree by those cards which he has
thrown during the early part of a hand when no tension was apparent. After the discard pile has begun
to bulge with wealth he is more likely to be trying to
deceive you by "fake" discards. A resourceful player
will, in such circumstances, frequently discard from
three or four or five of a kind, retaining a pair with
which to snatch the pile if you should throw a card
of the same denomination. Before either side has
made the initial meld it is the accepted practice to

toss low cards. Inasmuch as they count only five points each, they will not be of material assistance to the enemy in making up the count necessary for the first meld. It follows naturally that the discard of an Ace at a time like this is a rare spectacle, for, if picked up by the enemy it contributes substantially towards making up the required count, whereas a matching small card still leaves them some distance short of their goal.

If it becomes evident that you are due for some embarrassment in discarding and that sooner or later you will have to "give", bear in mind that it is better to throw dangerous cards when the up-pile is low, retaining those cards which appear to be somewhat safer for the time when the discard pile is bulging with wealth, and when ulcers begin to act up.

### THE BLACK THREE

In these times of tension, the black three takes a prominent role. As you are aware, the discard of a black three acts as a stop, and forces the next opponent to draw from the stock pile on that particular round, providing you with temporary relief. Since these cards can be a great source of comfort, they should not be thrown indiscriminately. When the discard of some useless card which appears to be reasonably safe, is available to you, you might as well keep the black three to use when the pressure is on. But it is not wise to clutter up your hand with black threes at the cost of building it up in a more constructive manner.

## MELDING ON COMPLETED CANASTA

Under the laws, the melding of additional cards on Canastas that have been completed is permitted. But whenever this is done, except as the player is going out, the practice is not at all recommended. All that one can gain by adding these additional melds is five, ten or twenty points, which in the general scheme of things should be ignored entirely. These cards may serve a far more useful purpose if kept for an emergency and they will be worth many times these points at a time when a safe discard is needed to prevent your left hand opponent from acquiring the discard pile.

These extra cards usually offer complete safety for it is rare indeed that your left hand opponent will have in his hand a natural pair of cards in which you have completed a Canasta. Of course, at a time when you are going out it is only natural that you when the enemy has a five card spread. Contributi

a sixth card to an enemy meld is undesirable for

places them within an eyelash of a Canasta.

When the opponents have reduced their hands to a very small number of cards after they have completed a Canasta, and it appears quite evident that they are playing to "go out", one should be very cautious in discarding to an empty table after having picked up the pile. The reason is very simple. If the card you throw "hits" your opponent, it may be the card that will put him out. If there are two or three cards in the discard pile at the time, this will not be such a serious matter for the two odd cards will very likely prevent the opponent from clearing his hand entirely, but where you have just picked up the pack, the discard pile will consist of only one card. If that is usable, you will in such cases very likely have put the opponent out. It is wise, therefore, not to throw "live cards" at such a time. The "live card" may be defined as one that has not heretofore made its appearance, so that there is a greater likelihood that your left hand opponent has a pair of them. This is the same type of tactics employed by the cautious gin player in the late stages of the game.

It may be interesting to look at a few cases in line with the technique of discarding. It is early in the

...ne and neither side has made its initial meld. Fifty
...ints are therefore required. There have been two
rounds of play and after the draw you hold:

### Joker-2-Q-Q-9-9-7-7-7-K-J-5

There is no good reason to postpone making the
initial meld. You should therefore spread the Joker
together with either the nines or the Queens. This is
the most economical manner in which it is possible
to go down inasmuch as three cards were consumed
in the process. Let us assume that you meld Joker-
Q-Q. (Notice that the Joker is employed for the purpose rather than the deuce.) Now you must discard.
The preceding plays may have made it evident that
you could safely discard the five, a card which can
do no good. However, you may practice a little chi-
canery by letting go a seven, and this is our recommended discard. This is no act of charity on your
part because you are giving away nothing of great
importance. There is this to be said on behalf of the
play. Your right hand opponent, if he is at all aware,
will make a mental note of the fact that you discarded a seven and if, as the play develops, discarding becomes painful to him and he is called upon to
make a guess as to the proper discard, he may choose
a seven in hope that you do not need such a card. If

such a contingency materializes you will, of course, be able to take up the discard pile and your "advertisement" will have shown very satisfactory results.

It will be seen that the discard of the seven, rather than the five, has not diminished your chances of obtaining the discard pile. Actually, it has improved those chances. If someone later on freezes the pack so that only natural pairs will permit you to go in, you will retain the same number of pairs which, of course, are indispensable at such time. If anyone freezes the pack, by retaining the five, you will have an additional chance of going in inasmuch as you have a deuce to help you use your neighbor's discard. In other words, you will be able to pick up the pile upon the discard of a Q-9-7-K-J or 5. Whereas, if you discard the five you will have one less chance.

Another example. The opponents have been busily engaged in building up various melds while your side has melded five fives and three Kings. After the draw you hold:

2-2-10-10-10-10 and 8-8-6-6-A-4

The suggested play is to meld one of your deuces on your string of fives. This is a conventional play which will be discussed in the next chapter requesting partner to build the Canasta with a wild card. You cannot hope that he has a five for surely he would have added it to your meld the last round if he had held one. Obviously, you will discard the four. Now, if your partner is able to complete a Canasta by the addition of a wild card you will be in a position to go out with a draw of a six, an eight, or a wild card. Or, if you draw a six, you will meld the three natural sixes or the two eights with the deuce and the four natural tens, and discard the Ace. If you draw an eight natural, meld three natural eights or pair the sixes with the deuce, the four tens and discard the Ace. If you draw a wild card, you will add one deuce to the eights making a legal meld, add one deuce to the sixes and the remaining wild card can be put down on either the six, the eight or the tens, leaving you again with the odd card to discard.

If you are not fortunate enough to draw a six or eight or a wild card, you still retain the deuce which keeps your hand in liquid condition for battle.

Another example. You need 90 points for your initial meld while your opponents need 120. It is very early in the game and in your hand you hold:

### Joker-A-K-K-10-9-7-7-7-6-6

You draw a five and you are not able to make your initial meld so you are obliged to discard. The question is, what card do you select for the purpose? Let us do this by the process of elimination. The Ace we eliminate forthwith. This card is not usually thrown early in the play because if it is usable by the opponents it is too valuable in helping to make up the 120 points for their initial meld. The recommended discard is the ten or the nine. You have no use for either of them. True enough, the five would seem to be a safer and more desirable discard at this point because of its lower value. But since the discard pile is not yet high, it seems that it would be more discreet to save it for a later round when the danger would be somewhat greater and you would be more concerned with safety.

By managing your hand in this fashion, you can pick up the pile and go down for the count of 90 if your right hand opponent happens to discard a six or seven and, though it is somewhat less likely, a King.

### THE CANASTA REQUEST CONVENTION

The partnership convention which is universally accepted is the request of partner to complete a Canasta. The request is made in the following fashion. Whenever a player adds a Joker or deuce to

a meld consisting of five cards, he pleads with partner to complete the Canasta by the addition of another wild card.

## FREEZING THE PACK
### (Making a Prize Pile)

One of the features which distinguishes Canasta
from all other rummy games is the unique practice
of freezing the discard pile. Freezing the pack has
the effect of vetoing the power of the wild cards, so
far as taking the discard pile is concerned. When
the pack is not frozen, it may be taken by a player
who holds a card which matches the last discard,
plus a deuce (to compose a three card meld). But
when the pack is frozen, the deuce and Joker may
not, during the freeze, be used for such purpose. In
order to go in, a player must have a natural pair to
match the last discard. When the pack is not frozen
a player may "go in" if the last discard is a card
which matches one of his own melds; such a card is
frequently called a "player". But during the freeze,
he may not go in for such a "player" unless he has a
natural pair to match it. A freeze is created during
the subsequent play when anyone discards a deuce
or a Joker. Such action is taken for the purpose of

making it more difficult for the opposition to take up the pile. It is particularly indicated when you hold cards which you know that the enemy can use (cards matching their melds) and your purpose is to restrict their sphere of action.

When you and your partner have a great many more cards than the opposing team, and each side has already made the initial meld, so that the pile is not frozen, you are in a strategic position to apply the freeze. It will be a considerably greater nuisance to them than to you. Because their hands have been depleted, it is reasonable to assume that they will find it difficult to put together pairs, so that their chances of going in will be negligible. Whereas you will find it much easier to accumulate a number of pairs and sooner or later the enemy will be obliged to part with a card to match one of them and the loot will be yours.

Observe an illustrative case:—You have not yet made your initial meld but the opponents have melded Queens, Jacks, tens and sixes. After drawing you hold:

2-Q-Q-J-J-10-10-10-8-8-8-4

The discard pile has reached desirable proportions and you are anxious to avoid giving it to them. You may not, therefore, discard a Q-J or 10. Your choice apparently narrows down to an eight or the four. You could get by, let us say, conveniently enough by letting go the four. But you will be faced with an awkward situation next time. To part with the eights would be to abandon your one hope to ultimately come through with a Canasta. The best play is the deuce, freezing the pile. This is sound strategy. It restricts the opposition without imposing an additional burden on you. For as far as you are concerned the pack is frozen anyway, since you have not made your first meld. If your right hand opponent throws a card to match one of your pairs you will obtain the pile. But what is more to the point, discarding will not now be a painful procedure.

Another example. Both sides need 120. The pile has grown to considerable height but it has not yet been frozen. All the players have been discarding small cards in an effort to prevent the opponents from attaining their required count of 120. Presently your left hand opponent makes his initial meld consisting of:

Joker-A-A        Q-Q-2

This consists of 130 points and is a legal initial meld. Your partner draws and discards as does your right

hand opponent, and now you find that your hand
consists of :

$$2\text{-A-A-Q-Q-Q-Q-K-K-10-10}$$

You draw another deuce. The required count could
be met by spreading the two deuces with the four
Queens and two Aces. You could make the legal
count for the initial meld but to do so would require
giving up the bulk of your hand, and you are
strongly advised against it. You have a splendid type
of hand designed for acquiring a frozen pack. In
other words, your hand contains four pairs. It would
therefore be to your advantage to impose this ob-
stacle in the race. It is highly doubtful that the opponents have as many pairs as you have. This would
give you a decided advantage if the pack were
frozen and you could bring that about by discarding
the deuce.

Your right hand opponent will almost surely be
obliged to play into your hand, whereas you will
have safe discards. It will be recalled that most of
the low cards have been consumed and your right
hand opponent is probably loaded down with high
ones so that in his discarding he will hardly be able
to escape you.

### TACTICS

As soon as partner makes his initial meld it is the practice of a great many players to add complimentary cards to partner's spread without delay. This is not always the soundest procedure. If you have an odd card which matches your partner's meld it is good policy to add it to him. But if you have a pair to match a meld spread by your partner you can obtain very gratifying results by holding on to it for a little while. This is especially true if you happen to be playing against an aggressive team. An aggressive team is very likely to freeze the pack in cases where you appear to be gaining the upper hand. If the pack becomes frozen, your right hand opponent will very likely consider it safe to throw cards of the rank melded by your side, for he will consider it unlikely that you hold a pair of that denomination without having added it to your partner's spread. This, of course, will give you possession of the pile and increase the advantage which you apparently have over your opponents. Generally speaking, it is important to have pairs because it permits you to prepare for either type of game, offensive or defensive. When the pack is frozen pairs are indispensable. If it becomes unfrozen it is easy to shift by splitting your pairs and holding a variety of cards.

However, the above advice should not be followed too slavishly. There is such a thing as being taken too literally. When your side has a meld which contains only three of your cards, it is expedient to add as quickly as possible a fourth natural card. The reason for this should be apparent. Until you have four natural cards in a meld you are not in position to complete a Canasta. This is a highly desirable position to achieve for without a Canasta you have learned that you are not permitted to go out. If the game begins to turn against you and the opponents appear to be well on their way to a big killing, your one hope may rest in the escape by way of going out so that it is desirable to be in a position where a Canasta can be completed readily and the escape made promptly.

Then, too, it is of considerable assistance to partner to have a fourth natural card placed upon his meld. He now knows which avenue to take in order to approach the nearest Canasta.

There should be no anxiety about adding a mere single card to your partner's meld if it will be only a third natural card. He may, for example, have melded 7-7-2 and you find yourself in possession of a single seven. There should be no haste to meld it. If an awkward situation develops you may find that it proves to be a useful discard to save you from the embarrassment of throwing something which your left hand opponent covets.

When a player has acquired a rich pile, he will surely be in position to spread a great many melds. Where one or more Canastas can be completed by the addition of natural cards, obviously the player should do so without any further delay. There is a tendency on the part of a great many players to add wild cards indiscriminately to melds in order to complete a Canasta. This is not sound policy and may prove to be a squandering of your assets. Wild cards should not be parted with so lightly. In this position a delay is indicated for one round unless, of course, you feel there is a grave danger that one of the opponents is apt to go out. During this delay of one round your partner will have the opportunity to complete these Canastas with natural cards if he is fortunate enough to have them. Now when he wants to do so you may distribute your wild cards in the most economical manner in the next round. In the development of the hand one cannot emphasize too strongly the principle that when the pack is frozen one must strive to retain as many pairs as possible.

When the pile is not frozen and the player possesses a wild card, it is to his advantage to have as many different cards as possible in his hand. This will make it almost impossible for his right hand opponent to discard something which he cannot take.

When the pile is frozen it is good policy to complete a Canasta immediately. This will put you in position to escape by going out as suggested above should the enemy begin to find things going all their own way. When the pack is frozen, therefore, it is sound economy to complete a Canasta even if it takes a couple of wild cards to do so. This is not the sacrifice that it might appear to be for it is plain to see that during the freeze wild cards are not nearly so important as they are at other times.

At this point it may be appropriate to refer again to the discarding convention which provides that when a player adds a wild card to a four or five card meld it is a request that his partner add another wild card to that meld as soon as possible. If, for example, you have melded Q-Q-Q-Q-Q and add a deuce or a Joker, converting it into a six card meld, your partner is conventionally being requested to complete the Canasta by adding a wild card of his own. A natural card would be preferable of course but that would be too much to hope for. If he had held a Queen on the previous round he would surely have added it to your five and made it six of a kind.

The convention also applies when you add a deuce to four of a kind. Your partner is expected to do likewise and if he happens to have two wild cards, too, he is expected to use them both for the purpose of completing the Canasta.

### DECEPTION

In the long run it will be profitable not to give too much information that can be useful to your right hand opponent. The less you tell him about the makeup of your hand the better off you are apt to be. And by the same token if you can palm off some misinformation you should not hesitate to do so. For example if you can in some way contrive to give him the impression that you are not interested in 7s you may profit by such a ruse. You may create this impression by discarding two 7s if you happen to be dealt four of them; this will leave you with a natural pair with which to snatch the pile if your right hand opponent can be pried loose of one of his 7s.

Another way in which the effect can be attained is with the holding of five of a kind, you may spread three of them and hold up a pair for later use. If someone freezes the pile you are an odds favorite to get one of this rank thrown to you by your right hand opponent.

Similarly when partner has made the initial meld it is not always good practice to add your cards to his melds immediately, especially if you have a pair of them. If you happen to be playing against opponents who are likely to freeze the pack these will be a great source of comfort when the pinch is on. Your right hand opponent is very apt to throw one of these cards in the belief that it is safe.

But when your side has a meld containing only three natural cards you should hasten to add a fourth natural, which will be a base for a future Canasta. Remember every Canasta must contain at least four cards.

A neat bit of deception that produced a gratifying result for my friend John Crawford, whom I was kibitzing at the Cavendish Club, is the following:

The deck was born frozen, that is, a deuce had been turned for the original up-card. Each side needed 90 for the initial meld and his opponents had already melded. After drawing he held:—

Joker-A-A-A-A-K-8-7-7-5-5-3

He melded the Joker with only two of the Aces. This is not the normal practice. With this holding most players would spread all four Aces, for partner might be able to complete the Canasta at once. He discarded the black three. Remember the discard pile was still frozen, the pile was growing and tension mounted. Crawford's right hand opponent threw as many safe cards as he could and finally decided that Crawford did not have a pair of Aces concealed and threw one. The acquisition of the pile gave his side an old-fashioned killing.

### GOING IN

Because a player can take up the discard pile it does not necessarily follow that he should do so. So much depends upon the character of the pile and the state of his hand. We rarely pass up an opportunity to go into the discard pile if we can do so with natural cards, but if it requires giving up one of our wild cards we prefer to do so in a good cause. In that case the discard pile should contain something of a distinct value.

We would not, for example, recommend the giving up of a deuce to picking up only two or three cards unless, of course, they were very important in the sense that a Canasta could be completed with them.

However, where discards have become onerous it may become desirable to go into the pile in order to pick up cards that will be convenient discards. At such times the fact that the pile contains some black 3s should be a considerable inducement. If they fall into the hand of your left hand neighbor he will have the advantage of safe discards, which may prove distasteful to your partner.

Let us examine an illustrative situation. Your opponents have spread melds consisting of Aces, Queens and 9s and a few other odds and ends; your hand, by reason of either bad luck or perhaps bad management, has been reduced to Ace, Queen and 9; your side has melded some 6s and at this time the discard pile is very small, and contains nothing very glamorous; your right hand opponent now discards a 6. Our suggestion would be to go in, for if you should draw instead and pick a card which is embarrassing you will have no reasonable discard to make, but if you pick up the pile you will have some nondescript cards in your hand which will provide you with safe discards and protect you from the pressure of a squeeze.

But in the following example we would not recommend going in: Your side has melded

A-A-A-Q-Q-Q-Q-10-10-10-2

Your holding consists of

2-A-J-J-6

At this point your right hand opponent discards a 6, an obviously dangerous card; presumably he has done so because there is not a big discard pile. If there were you would naturally go in, but on the other hand he might not have thrown the 6. You could naturally take up the pile by using your deuce and 6 to match the up card, but it would be doubtful strategy to do so. You would be insufficiently compensated for parting with your only deuce. Furthermore, passing up the 6 may prove to be a good investment for your right hand opponent, not knowing that you have a concealed 6, may try his luck with the discard of a 6 later on when the pile is more attractive and it will be worth while to give up your deuce.

GOING OUT

Another distinctive feature of the game of Canasta is the practice of consulting with partner when it is the desire of one of them to go out. He has the privilege of asking, "May I go out, partner?" The asking is not prescribed. If a player wishes to go out without consulting the partner he is at perfect liberty to do so. Failure to ask partner is not looked upon as a slur upon his powers of judgment nor is it a violation of social amenities. Where partner has a great many cards, it behooves you to consult him, especially if you have some five or six card melds in front of you. If he is in position to complete some of them he will naturally refuse your request and you may repeat the request on subsequent rounds if you have been turned down before.

Where the opponents have not yet melded and you are quite convinced that the partnership interest will best be served by going out, do not ask partner's permission.

You should be quick to go out when the opponents have spread three red treys and you have none. It is in their interest to continue the game, so that they will have an opportunity to draw the fourth red trey.

On the same line of reasoning, where your side has three red treys, lean in favor of continuing the game, when a real doubt exists.

As distinct from games like Oklahoma and Gin, there is no great importance attached to the act of going out. There is only a 100 point bonus for going out on a particular deal, which does not weigh heavily in the scale. Remember, too, that while the game ends when one side passes 5000 points there is no bonus for getting there. It just marks the time when play ceases and the score is added. The winning team is the one with the most points.

Your policy in the late stages of the game will frequently be dictated by the state of the score, and it is good practice to make a rough estimate of the amount of your current melds to help determine what the score would be if the game ended at any time.

If you can so time the play that you will go out with a score of about 2800, it is desirable to do so where it appears that there is little likelihood of your building more than one additional Canasta. For if you continue play and go out with a score of 3100 you will need 120 for your initial meld on the next deal. Whereas, if you stay below 3000, you will need only 90. The difference between 90 and 120 is simply enormous and it is worth sacrificing a probable Canasta to gain this advantage on the next deal.

Similarly it would be poor policy to go out when your score is almost but not quite 5000. Stick it out for the few more points that will put you over the line.

"Going out" is frequently done in self-defense. Where the opponents appear to have the upper hand and you evidently have no future, your one refuge may be in going out. In this situation you should follow the technique of the gin players and keep the greatest number of combinations that will permit your going out, and this even at the expense of deliberately giving the enemy a Canasta or two.

The following is an illustration in point:

Both sides need 120. Opponents have not melded, whereas your side has melded:

A-A-A-Joker-A     K-K-Joker-K     Q-Q-Q

You hold 2-A-K-Q-3 and you draw a King. You may, if you choose, complete a Canasta of Aces by adding the Ace and the deuce to your meld. By then melding the two Kings and the Queen, you may go out by discarding the three.

But you are advised against going out. There is little doubt that you can roll up a big score and it is improbable that the opponents will be able to make their initial meld for some time since you have two of the Jokers and five of the Aces.

You should not be satisfied with a small profit. Do not close up shop. Stay in business. The winning Canasta player gathers his rosebuds while he may.

# IV

# Canasta for Two, Three, Five or Six Players

In the two hand game each player is dealt 15 cards.

The requirements regarding the initial meld are the same as in the four hand game, but the strategy is quite different. In the partnership game the importance of making an early initial meld was emphasized. Such action provided relief for partner, who no longer had to concern himself with so managing his hand as to make the required count. But in this type of game, where you have no partner, with whom to concern yourself, there is no such urgency to make the first meld. It is true that the initial meld unfreezes the pack for you and permits you to go in with the aid of a wild card, but the advantage in this respect is slight. It will, however, have the effect of more or less compelling your adversary to part with a wild card in order to freeze the pack.

It is of the utmost importance to keep your opponent guessing as to the nature of your hand. It is, therefore, basic in the strategy of the 2 handed game, that one should not meld except to take the discard pile.

In such cases a player should meld only what he must from his own hand. There is no special advantage in concealing melds that you picked up in the discard pile, for presumably your opponent knows what it contained and in that respect you cannot keep him in the dark.

Melding three or four of a kind during the course of the game is not recommended unless you retain in your hand natural pairs matching those melds. The purpose is to enable you to go into the pile in times of stress.

If, in picking up the discard pile, you acquired three nines, having, in the concealed hand, two more nines, by no means should you meld five of them, though there is no objection to melding three since your opponent knows that you have them. But you must retain a pair concealed. When the pressure is on and the pack is frozen, your adversary may reach the conclusion that a 9 is a safer discard than some other that he is contemplating and this may permit you to annex a rich pile.

In the two hand game, a player may not go out without first having completed two Canastas. Inasmuch as only 15 cards are dealt to each player it is evident, therefore, that one can hardly go out without having gone in for a well nourished pack at some time or other.

It becomes clear that the importance of protecting the discard pile is even more pronounced than in the four hand game. If your opponent never succeeds in getting the pack, you may discount his chances of ever accumulating two Canastas. One, therefore, should not be inclined to take too many chances in the early part of the game, and should discard with an eye to safety.

When your opponent requires 120 points for his initial meld you will naturally refrain from throwing him Aces, which may contribute substantially to his cause, choosing instead the lower cards, which count only 5 points each. Generally speaking the safest discards are those he has thrown, though you must not be too greatly surprised if he has been engaging in a little "come-on" game to coax that discard out of you. But it is the best percentage play.

This method of "safe" discarding should be resorted to after the discard pile has begun to bulge. In the earlier stages when the pile is not yet enriched, it is sound policy to toss cards of somewhat lesser safety, for if you happen to strike him then the loot will not be so heavy.

*Freezing:* Freezing the pack is apt to occur with greater frequency in the two hand game. If your opponent has made his first meld before you have, he enjoys a considerable advantage over you, in that he does not need a natural pair to "go in". Since the pack remains frozen to you but not to him, it is good practice for you to equalize matters by tossing a deuce into the pile and freezing it for him as well. If at the time the pack is frozen to you, but not to him, you happen to have an assortment of black threes, keep pitching them, for as long as they last your adversary cannot go in, but as soon as the supply is exhausted you should discard a wild card, even if it is your only one. This is not too high a price to pay for the privilege of staving off, at least temporarily, an enemy "pick up".

### THREE HAND CANASTA

The rules for the two and four handed game apply. The player who cuts the highest card has his choice of seats. The player who cuts the lowest card sits to his right and deals the first hand to him. Thirteen cards are dealt to each player.

At the conclusion of the game, the player with the highest score collects from both opponents. The player with the second best score collects from the player with the lowest score. The latter practice, however, may be varied by agreement. That is to say, the players may agree beforehand that there is to be but one winner.

The question of—What to do with that extra man (or woman if you prefer) has plagued many a hostess. She need fret no longer, for they can manage to engage in:—

### CANASTA FOR FIVE PLAYERS

In this type of game the two who cut the high cards form a team and compete against the remaining three. The team of three has two active players for each hand, with one remaining out, and the players each take turns at staying out.

*Variation for Five Players:* There is an interesting variation of the game for five players, in which each one plays on his own account:—

The five players cut, the two cutting the highest cards become partners against the two cutting the next highest cards. The one cutting the low card remains out the first deal. The players each take a turn out, and the order is determined by the original cut.

The player remaining out becomes a member of

one of the teams (some players give the outside member the choice of teams, but in our opinion the sounder procedure is to have this question determined by cutting another card for the purpose, e.g., if the specially cut card is a red one the fifth player becomes a member of one team, if it is a black one, he joins the other team). The fifth player may not be consulted. At the conclusion of the hand he receives the same score as each active member of his team.

The partnership pivot is executed in the following manner:—the player who has just been out returns and takes the seat of the player who is making his exit. The person to the left of the incomer remains in the same seat, and the other two exchange places. Let us observe how this operates with a series of diagrams:

It is the first deal and E has cut the lowest card, so he is out the first hand. A and B have cut the highest cards so the seating arrangement is as follows:

                    C
          A     1     B
                    D
            (Dealer)          E sits out.

E cuts a card and announces "If it is a red card I will join A and B, if it is a black card I will join C and D". He turns a red card and becomes a silent partner in the firm of A and B.

At the end of the deal A and B have +1280 points, C and D +850. The score sheet now reads:—

A    +1280
B    +1280
C    +850
D    +850
E    +1280

It is now time for the second hand and it is D's turn out. E, who has just been out takes D's place. A, to the left of the incomer remains in the same seat and the other two exchange places. D, who is now out, draws a card to determine which side he will be on. He becomes a member of the A-C team and the seating arrangement is:—

B

A    2    C

E                    D sits out.

On this hand E-B score 950 points and A-C score 610.

The score sheet now reads:—

A    +1890
B    +2230
C    +1460
D    +1460
E    +2230

The third deal is coming up. It is C's turn out and D, who has just sat out, takes his place. E, to the left of the incomer, remains seated, and the other two exchange places. C, who is out, draws a card to see which side he will join. He becomes a member of B-D team and the seating arrangement is:—

A
B    3    D
E              C sits out

Now for the initial meld on this deal. E has 2230 and A has 1890, so clearly the initial meld requirement for their side is 90 points because they are both over 1495.

B's score is 2230 which makes his requirement for the initial meld 90 points. His partner, D, has only 1460 and would, therefore, normally need only 50 (seated two seats away). In the diagram shown above—

> B-1 would inquire of B-2
> B-2 would inquire of B-3
> B-3 would inquire of B-1.

If the player, of whom the inquiry is made, undertakes to answer his reply is binding on the team. And he must reply simply "Yes" or "No". But if that player prefers not to make the decision, he may pass it to the remaining member of the team. However, in so doing he must not engage in any oratory, by way of qualifying phrases. He must say simply "I pass". The decision must then be made by the remaining member of the team, and it is final. However, as in the four hand game, the question may be repeated on subsequent rounds.

Because of the very nature of this game with more than half the cards dealt on the first round and with three players contributing jointly to the building of melds, it is natural that the game should move along at a more rapid pace, and that the stockpile should be more quickly exhausted. It is important, therefore, to go in for the discard pile as often as possible even if it contains only four or five cards.

The practice of holding up melds for deceptive purposes is not recommended in the six hand game. But one should emphasize the importance of making the initial meld as soon as possible. In the four hand game, we cautioned against depleting your hand too drastically, and recommended that the initial meld be postponed for a round or two, where the initial meld would take too many cards out of your hand. This advice is not applicable to the six hand game. The initial meld should be made at the very first possible opportunity. You may no longer be a prominent factor in the game but you will have acted in a good cause, and you will have two partners who will be able to carry on for you. Your initial meld will have been in the nature of a sacrifice bunt in baseball, made for the purpose of advancing your team mates.

*Variation of Six Hand Canasta:* There is a variation of the game for six players which is less popular than the others but preferred by some players.

The teams are selected as in the other form of the game. Those drawing the three high cards form a team against the other three.

However, only two players on each team engage in the actual play of any hand. The player on each team who has drawn the lowest card remains inactive on the first deal, and the players keep rotating, each taking a turn out.

The inactive player has no rights and may not be consulted by his team-mates. The inactive player, however, has the right to draw attention to errors in the scoring at the conclusion of a deal.

# V

# The Conduct of Canasta Tournaments

The most interesting form of contest is a tournament for pairs (two on a team). There are various methods by which tournaments may be conducted and we shall consider those that enjoy the greatest popularity.

## MITCHELL MOVEMENT
### (*Total Points*)

In order to describe this method let us assume that we have ten tables in play, that is twenty pairs (forty individual persons). The players take seats which are arbitrarily designated as North-South and East-West. These directions, of course, have no bearing whatsoever on the true geographical directions. It is customary, however, to treat the long axis of the room as North-South and the shorter as East-West.

The tables are numbered from one to 10. The

North-South pairs take their numbers from the table at which they are seated, so that they are numbered respectively 1 to 10 in that order. The East-West pair that starts at table 1 is designated as team 11, the pair at table 2 as team 12 and so on up to 20.

If there were only 6 tables in play the North-South pairs would be designated as teams 1 to 6, and the East-West pairs would be numbered from 7 to 12.

Pairs occupying the North-South seats remain in the same places throughout the contest, whereas, at the end of each match the East-West pairs move to the next higher numbered table. From table one to table two, from table two to table three, and so on. The East and West pair seated at the highest numbered table progress to table one, etc.

A complete game is played by one pair against the other pair. It will readily be seen that it would not be possible to complete the movement in one sitting if you had ten tables. For, even if play proceeded with more than normal rapidity you could not hope to play 10 games. The solution to the problem lies in either dividing the players into smaller sections, let us say 4 or 5 tables to a section, or conducting the contest in several sessions. Another solution is to curtail play by setting a time limit, but this is the least satisfactory.

The most practical method for speeding up the action is to start all teams with a score of 1500 points (the initial meld requirement would, of course, be 90 points).

After a game has been completed the result of the match, and the exact score, are recorded on a score slip and turned in to the tournament director. The score slip may be improvised, and reads simply Team #2 defeated Team #8 by 1475 points. Team #2 is, therefore, plus 1475 points and Team #8 is minus 1475 points. The master score sheet on page 108 shows how the score might look at the end of three matches.

The winners are Mr. & Mrs. Jones with +2185. The runners up are Mr. & Mrs. Williams with +895. In third place Mr. & Mrs. Brown with a score of —70.

It will be observed that Team #5 (Mr. & Mrs. Williams) won all three of their matches, but their aggregate score was only 895 points and they could do no better than finish second. Whereas Team #2 (Mr. & Mrs. Jones) lost two matches and were victorious in only one, yet they won the contest handily.

There are many persons who do not regard this

## RECAPITULATION SHEET

| Team No. | 1st Match | 2nd Match | 3rd Match | Net Score | Rank |
|---|---|---|---|---|---|
| 1. Mr. & Mrs. Brown | +1450 | —1100 | —420 | —70 | 3 |
| 2. Mr. & Mrs. Jones | —375 | —80 | +2640 | +2185 | 1 |
| 3. Mr. & Mrs. Smith | +720 | —100 | —900 | —280 | |
| 4. Mr. & Mrs. Roberts | —1450 | +80 | +900 | +470 | |
| 5. Mr. & Mrs. Williams | +375 | +100 | +420 | +895 | 2 |
| 6. Mr. & Mrs. Harris | —720 | +1100 | —2640 | —2260 | |

method of scoring as the most equitable. Their argument is that the entire contest may be determined by one or two pivotal hands. There is considerable merit in their contention and the modern tendency in this form of competition (in all games, particularly BRIDGE) is to have the contest scored on a match play basis.

### MITCHELL MOVEMENT
#### (*Match points*)

In this method the winner of each match receives a point. And the pair with the most points at the conclusion of the contest is declared the winner.

Scored in this fashion the contest illustrated above would have ended as follows:—

Mr. & Mrs. Williams (Team #5) would have won the contest with three matches: Mr. & Mrs. Roberts (Team #4) would have finished second with two matches; and there would have been a four way tie for third place with one match each. This tie would have been broken on a total point basis, and Mr. & Mrs. Jones, with plus 2185 would have finished in third place.

There are many who consider that this is not altogether fair, because no recognition whatever is given to the margin of victory. There is a compromise method:—

One point is awarded for winning a match by any margin up to 1200 points, if the match is won by more than this margin the winner is credited with two points.

Scored in this manner Mr. & Mrs. Williams (Team ⧣5) would still be the winner, having won three 1 point matches (margin of victory less than 1200 points) or a total of 3 points. There would be a three way tie for second, with 2 points each, between Mr. & Mrs. Brown (Team ⧣1) who scored one two-point victory, Mr. & Mrs. Jones (Team ⧣2) who scored one two-point victory and Mr. & Mrs. Roberts (Team ⧣4) who scored two one-point victories. The tie would be broken on a basis of total points, and Mr. & Mrs. Jones, with plus 2185 would be declared the runner-up.

## ELIMINATION TOURNAMENT

There are various ways to manage a tournament of this kind. The most popular is the one fashioned after the tennis tournament—or match play at golf.

It works best where the number of teams represents a power of 4. That is 32—16—8—4. Assuming the larger number, on the first round sixteen teams are pitted against the other sixteen. The losing teams are eliminated and on the second round eight teams play against the remaining eight with the losers being eliminated from the tournament and so on, until only two teams remain and they play off for the crown. In order to determine the pairings for each match, it is suggested that the names of the contestants be placed on a score sheet of the type furnished by the leading sportsgoods manufacturers. The bracket for eight teams would look like this.

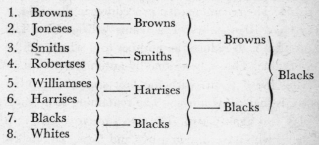

Mr. & Mrs. Black were the winners, having defeated the Browns in the finals, the Harrises in the semi-finals and the Whites in the first round (or the round of 8 usually called the quarter-finals).

Where players are more or less evenly balanced, the post positions are drawn out of a hat. But where there are varying degrees of talent, it is accepted practice to "seed" the players, so that those who are considered the best on form will meet in the later rounds. This is done as follows:—The best team takes ⚹1. The next best ⚹8 (or ⚹16 if that happens to be the highest number). The next best is ⚹3 and the next ⚹6, and so on.

It is customary to have a special consolation tournament for those who have been eliminated in the first round.

The problem will frequently arise as to the handling of inconvenient numbers, such as, let us say, 20 teams. The recommended procedure, in that case, is to have 10 matches. Ten teams will survive. The problem is to reduce the number to 8 which will be workable. This is best done by automatically qualifying the 6 teams with the best scores. (In other words they draw a bye.) The remaining four teams play two against two. The two survivors join with the 6, who have drawn a bye and form the bracket of eight to follow through as indicated above.

## ARGENTINE TYPE
### ELIMINATION TOURNAMENT

The distinguishing feature of this type of tournament is that all teams survive the first round and are not eliminated from the contest unless they lose the second round. At the end of the first round the winning teams go into Section A—the losing teams make up Section B.

Thereafter, and until the final match, players remain in their own section. The seating positions are assigned by the tournament director. The pairs that lose in the second round are eliminated from the tournament. The process of elimination is continued in the subsequent rounds until only one pair is left in each section. These two pairs then play for the championship.

In the final match should the Section A team win they are declared the champions. If the Section B team should win there is further action. The reason is, at this point, each team has won all its games but one, so a theoretical tie is presumed to exist. This necessitates a play-off game and the winner is declared champion.

Where, during the elimination rounds, the numbers are unworkable a sufficient number of players are awarded a "bye" in order to bring the number down to 16, 8, or 4.

# VI

## The Laws of Canasta

## THE GAME

(1) Canasta is a rummy type game. The game ends when either or both sides have scored a total of 5000 points, but is never concluded before the completion of the current hand.

The winner and the margin of victory are determined by taking the difference between the scores of the two teams at the end of play. Thus Team A has a total of 5120 points, whereas Team B has amassed 5870. Team B is the winner by 750 points.

## THE PLAYERS

(2) Canasta may be played as a game for various numbers of participants. There is the two handed game—three handed game—the game for four hands and the game for six hands. The five handed game is really a variation of the game for four players.

When there are two or three players, each one

plays for himself. Four players divide into two opposing partnerships. Six players divide into two partnerships, with three members on each team. Partners occupy alternate positions around the table, so that a player is always seated between two opponents.

When there are five players, one team consists of two and the other of three. One of the three members sits out each hand, and these players rotate among themselves in such fashion that each one takes a turn out. But they each have a one-third interest in the partnership venture.

### THE CARDS

(3) The game of Canasta is played with a pack consisting of two full decks of standard playing cards, to which are added four Jokers, making in all a pack of 108 cards.

### THE DEAL

(4) (a) Players cut for partners, for choice of seats and for deal.

For purposes of the cut the Ace is the highest card,

followed by the King and so on down to the deuce, which is low. The Joker in this case counts for nothing. If a player, in cutting, draws a Joker his draw is void and he cuts another card.

If two players draw cards of the same size, the tie is broken on the basis of suit ranks. The suits rank as follows:

(1) Spades        (2) Hearts
(3) Diamonds     (4) Clubs

If two players draw identical cards, that is, cards of the same size in the same suit (e.g., two 10s of Diamonds or two Queens of Clubs) they must draw again to break the tie, as between those two players. Their tie, and the manner in which it is broken, does not affect the position of the two other players who have cut.

(b) The player who cuts the highest card has the choice, and the player who has cut the second highest card becomes his partner and of course sits opposite to him. The other two players take the remaining seats.

(c) The player who cuts the highest card has the privilege of making the first play. Therefore, the opponent who occupies the seat to his right becomes dealer. After the first deal the turn to deal passes clockwise (to the left) and so forth for ensuing deals, if there are any.

All players have the right to shuffle, but the final shuffle is the prerogative of the dealer. And the privilege of cutting the cards before the deal belongs to the player on the dealer's right. When the cut is made each packet must contain at least four cards.

(d) At the conclusion of a game the players may either (1) cut again, or (2) change partners, in accordance with the agreement of the parties at the start of play. If no prior agreement has been made, then partners for the next game are determined by cutting. Where it is agreed to change partners at the conclusion of a game (the pivot) it is good practice for the dealer and his left hand opponent to remain in their places, while the other two change seats. For the third game the dealer remains in his place, and takes for his partner the person with whom he has not yet played. At the end of this game, the pivot has been completed and the players cut again, as at the start of the play.

(e) Eleven cards are dealt, one at a time, to each player, starting with the player at the dealer's left and proceeding in a clockwise direction. The 45th card is faced upon the table and is called the "up-card". The remaining cards are called the stock and are placed on the table adjacent to the up-card. If the up-card happens to be a red three, a Joker or a deuce, the dealer must cover it with the next card from the stock pile. This process is repeated if necessary until a natural card, that is, some card other than one of the three special cards mentioned above is turned up.

A player may not look at or pick up his cards until the deal has been completed. The deal begins with the completion of the cut and ends when a proper up-card has been turned up.

(f) Each player at his first turn to play (but not before) is given the opportunity to expose any red threes that may have been dealt to him, and they are placed face upward on the table in front of him or his partner. Such player replaces such red threes by drawing the top card of the stock pile in order to replenish his hand. If he should happen to have been dealt two or more red threes he exposes them all and draws enough cards from the stock pile to bring the number of cards in his hand up to the required eleven. If he should draw another red three, he likewise exposes it and draws again from the stock pile to replenish his hand.

(g) The player to the left of the dealer has the

option of taking the up-card, if he is legally able to
do so, or of drawing from the stock pile. The privilege of taking the up card on the deal does not pass
to the other players.

### DEAL OUT OF TURN

(5) Before the first play, if it is discovered that the
cards were not dealt by the proper player, the deal
nevertheless stands, but the first play is made by the
person whose turn it would have been to play if the
proper player had dealt. It is then presumed that
the proper player actually dealt the cards, and for
the following hand the deal progresses as though the
proper person had dealt.

If, after the beginning of the first play, it is discovered that the cards were not dealt by the proper
player, the deal stands and play continues as though
no irregularity had been committed. On the next
hand the deal progresses to the left of the person who
actually dealt the cards. For example: It is right-
fully East's deal, but South deals in error. The deal
is completed and West draws and while he is think-
ing of a discard it is discovered that South dealt in
error. The deal nevertheless stands and play proceeds. The next hand will be dealt by West.

### NEW DEAL

(6) (*a*) There must be a new deal if it is discovered before the completion of the deal, that the cards were not cut.

(*b*) There must be a new deal if, during the deal, the dealer exposes any card other than the proper up-card.

(*c*) There must be a new deal if, before each player has made his first play, it is discovered that any player was dealt an incorrect number of cards. But if the discovery is made after each player has made his first play, the play continues, as though no irregularity had occurred.

(*d*) There must be a new deal if, before each player has made his first play, a card is found faced in the stock, or if a card from some other deck is found either in the pack or in some player's hand, or if it is discovered that a card is missing.

But if such discovery is made after each player has made his first play, a faced card is turned and shuffled with the rest of the stock, a card from some other deck is removed, and if it was taken from a player's hand, that player replaces the card with one taken from the top of the stock pile. A missing

card, when it is found, is shown to all the players
and set aside until the next deal. If the missing card
cannot be found, play continues, but a complete
deck must be substituted for the next deal. However,
the scores of all hands that have previously been
played with an improper deck, stand as official and
may not be corrected.

### THE BONUSES AND SCORING

(7) The following is the table of bonuses:—

| | |
|---|---|
| Canasta (*natural*) | 500 points each |
| Canasta (*mixed*) | 300 points each |
| Red Threes (*if all four are held by the same team*) | 200 points each |
| Red Threes (*if less than four are held*) | 100 points each |
| Melding out | 100 points |
| Concealed hand bonus | 100 points |

(*a*) At the conclusion of each hand the bonus
points are first added (this includes the bonuses for
Canastas, red threes, and for melding out). This
total is called the base. To the base is added the
value of all cards included in Canastas and other
melds. (Note that in addition to the Canasta bonus

a side receives credit for the cards which made up that Canasta.)

(*b*) From the combined total there is deducted the value of cards left in the players' hands. Cards remaining in a player's hand must be paid for even though they could have been melded.

It is at this time that the deduction should be made for any penalty incurred by a side.

(*c*) The game continues until one side's total score at the end of a hand exceeds 5000 points. Each hand is played to the end even though the 5000 goal has been reached during the play. In case both sides score more than 5000 points the one with the greatest number of points is the winner.

(*d*) The score becomes official when it has been agreed upon and recorded, but errors in arithmetic must be corrected. If an error in addition or subtraction is discovered after the next deal has started, but before the first draw has been made, it should be corrected at once, if it will affect the amount which either side will require for its initial meld. If the error is discovered after some one has drawn to the next deal, the correction is not made at once, but after the conclusion of the deal; even though the error would affect the amount which either side would require for the initial meld.

If a new game has been started as a result of an error in addition or subtraction (i.e., the game would not have been over if the arithmetic had been correct) the new game nevertheless proceeds, and the old game is completed afterward. Provided, however, that if any of the participants in the first game has left, the score stands as official.

### THE PLAY

(8) The person to the left of the dealer makes the first play. Each one then plays in proper turn, proceeding in a clockwise direction. Each play consists of three parts:

1—The Draw
2—The Meld (*This is optional. A player need not meld if he does not choose to do so.*)
3—The Discard.

The player to the left of the dealer begins play by drawing the top card of the stock or the up card. (9) As soon as a player touches either a card in the up pile or the stock he must take it (assuming he is legally able to take the up pile). This does not apply to cards that have been accidentally touched or touched while in the act of arranging cards in an orderly fashion.

(10) After drawing, a player may meld if he is able to, provided he so desires, but he must, of course, meld if he takes the up card. The player MUST then make a discard, except that a discard is not compulsory if he melds out legally.

The discard is placed directly on top of the previous discards, so that only the last card may be seen. It is not permitted to look at any cards in the discard pile other than the one on top.

### THE DRAW

(11) Each player in his proper turn may draw the top card of the stock pile and add it to his hand, or he may draw the discard pile, if he is able to meet certain requirements, which will be herein outlined.

(12) For the purpose of the partnership's first meld a player may take the discard pile, only if he has two cards matching the up card and sufficient amount to meet the requirements for the initial meld. The up card, but no other card in the up pile, may count toward making up the initial meld (See law for Initial Meld).

(13) Whenever the top card of the discard pile is used for a meld, the cards beneath it, that is, the entire discard pile, must be taken with it. These cards

become the property of the player who picks them up and he may meld them at the time or reserve his right to meld them at a later time. But the up card must be melded.

(14) A player must expose the cards to be melded from his hand before taking the up pile.

(15) After a player or his partner has made the initial meld, he may take the up pile when the up card matches a concealed pair, or when the up card matches one natural and a wild card, which may be used as the third card of the meld. A player, whose side has already made its initial meld, may take the discard pile when the up card can be added to one of his exposed melds (For this purpose, a closed Canasta is the same as any other meld.), except where the discard pile is frozen (a prize pile).

(16) The up card may never be taken to play with only two or more wild cards.

(17) A player who holds only one card in his hand may not take a discard pile consisting of only one card, unless the stock is exhausted.

(18) The taking of the up pile is optional with the player. Even though he may meld the up card he may elect to draw from the stock pile.

(19) The discard pile is frozen (a prize pile) when it contains a red three, or a wild card. At such time

it may be taken only by a player who is able to produce two natural cards of the same rank as the top card. It may not be taken with one matching card and a wild card. Nor may it be taken merely because the up card is playable on an exposed meld, unless the player has two more such cards concealed in his hand. (If a partnership has not yet melded the minimum count requirement must also be met.)

## THE MELD

(20) A meld consists of three or more cards of the same rank (without regard to suits) which are spread upon the table in the course of a player's proper turn to play. Sequences have no significance, and do not constitute a meld.

(21) A player is permitted to make more than one meld, whenever it is his turn to play; that is to say, he may spread any number of groups of the same rank. For example, he may meld simultaneously, 3 Aces, 3 tens, 4 nines, etc.

(22) When a meld is being made, a wild card (Joker or deuce) may be used as a card of any rank, with the proviso that a meld must contain at least two natural cards, and may not include more than three wild cards, except as provided in law 33.

(23) The melds contributed by members of the same team are pooled and for the sake of simplicity they are kept in front of one of the partners without regard as to which one contributed the meld.

(24) The following is the scale of values for cards melded:

| | |
|---|---|
| Jokers (*regardless of what card they represent*) | 50 points |
| Deuces (*regardless of what card they represent*) | 20 points |
| Aces | 20 points |
| All high cards (K-Q-J-10-9-8) | 10 points |
| All low cards (7-6-5-4 and black 3) | 5 points |

Black threes may not be melded during the ordinary course of play, but only at the end when a player is melding out on that turn to play.

(25) *The Initial Meld:* The initial meld of a partnership may be made only when the cards included in that meld have a combined value of certain specified points, depending upon the state of the score, at the beginning of the deal. After a team reaches certain stages in the score, stricter requirements are imposed upon it for the initial meld, and this is without regard for what the opponents' score may be at the time.

(26) The following is the scale of requirements for making the initial meld:

| When a team's score is: | Their required initial meld is: |
|---|---|
| Minus | 15 points |
| 0 to 1495 | 50 points |
| 1500 to 2995 | 90 points |
| 3000 or more | 120 points |

To meet these requirements a player may spread more than one group of matching cards, provided they are melded at one time. To make up the minimum count for the initial meld, the top card of the discard pile (provided, of course, the player has a natural pair in his hand to match it) may be used. But no other card in the discard pile may be used for the purpose of making up the minimum count.

(27) A player proposing to take up the discard pile for his initial meld must first establish his right to do so by spreading face up on the table, all the cards which will be used to make up the required count. Before showing such cards, it is improper for a player to touch the discard pile.

(28) For the purpose of the partnership's first meld, the discard pile may be taken only if the player is able to show two or more cards of the same rank

as the top of the discard pile, and is able to meet the minimum requirement in count.

(29) When one partner has made an initial meld, the other partner too is relieved of the restriction, and either partner may add cards to their exposed melds. After the initial meld, either partner may, when it is his turn to play, take the discard pile with two or more cards of the same rank as the top card of the discard pile, or with one such card and a wild card.

(30) If the top card of the discard pile matches a meld already made, by a player or his partner, he may take the pile and add it to his meld. The latter provision, however, does not apply when the discard pile is frozen (i.e., it contains a red three or a wild card).

(31) A player who holds only one card in his hand may not take a discard pile consisting of only one card unless the stock is exhausted, in which case he must do so, if able to.

(32) Black threes may be melded only by a player who is melding out on that turn to play. For that purpose two black threes and a wild card (or three or four black threes) may be used.

(33) A Canasta is a meld composed of seven cards of the same rank. They need not be melded at once,

but may be accumulated gradually. At least four of the cards in a Canasta must be natural. A Canasta may include more than three wild cards if:
(a) the meld includes at least four natural cards;
(b) the count of the additional wild cards is not used in reaching the minimum count required for the first meld.

(34) For the purpose of the meld, a wild card may take the place of a natural card but always retains its own value, when the cards are being counted at the end of the hand for the purpose of recording the score (e.g., 6-6-2 counts thirty points, twenty for the deuce even though it represents a 6, and five points for each of the sixes).

(35) When a wild card is designated as part of a meld, it is a permanent part of that meld and may not be substituted later on for the natural card, after which it was named.

(36) When a Canasta has been completed the partners may continue to add cards of the same rank. These additional cards are included in the count of melded cards, at the conclusion of the hand but they have no effect upon the bonus for the Canasta, which remains the same.

(37) Wild cards may be added to a closed Canasta, but if a wild card is added to a closed NAT-

URAL Canasta (which would take place only when it is the desire of a player to go out and he has no other meld upon which to place the wild card) the Canasta becomes converted to a MIXED Canasta.

(38) When a Canasta is completed the cards are folded together and piled in a stack. For purposes of identification a red card is left on top of a NAT-URAL Canasta, and a black card on top of a mixed Canasta. This is not mandatory, if a card of the indicated color is not available other means of identification must be employed.

(39) There is a bonus of 500 points for a natural Canasta, and a bonus of 300 points for a mixed Canasta, containing from one to three wild cards.

(40) Play ceases when any player melds every card in his hand. This is known as "going out". A player in going out is permitted to make a final discard but he is not obligated to do so. In other words, a player may go out by melding all his cards but one, which he may discard.

(41) In order to be eligible to "go out" a player's side must have previously completed a Canasta, or must be able to complete one in the act of melding out.

(42) A player may not discard all his cards with-

out melding out. The side that melds out receives a bonus of 100 points for "going out".

(43) "A concealed hand" is one with which a player goes out without having previously melded. That is to say, he melds out his complete hand at one turn. The player must naturally meld a Canasta to be eligible to go out. There is a bonus of 100 points in addition to the 100 point bonus for going out, if a player melds a concealed hand without adding any cards to his partner's meld.

(44) The minimum requirement for the initial meld does not apply when a player is able to go out with a concealed hand. (For example: The team composed of A and B need 120 points for their initial meld. A has not yet melded and B, his partner, suddenly finds that he can meld his entire hand, including a Canasta, and go out; but his cards are all small ones and he cannot count 120. He is, nevertheless, permitted to go out, for the restriction as to the first meld, does not apply in this case.)

(45) At his proper turn to play, a player may add cards from his hand to previous melds of the partnership. He may not, however, add cards to the melds of his opponents.

## THE DISCARD

(46) When a player has completed his play he must discard one card from his concealed hand except when he melds out, in which case the discard is optional.

(47) When a player discards a black three the next player may not take the discard pile at that turn, but subsequent plays are not affected by the circumstance that the discard pile contains a black three.

(48) After discarding, when a player is left with only one card, he may announce it to the other players.

At his own turn to play, any player may exercise the privilege of inquiring of any other player at the table, how many cards he has in his concealed holding. This question may be asked of partner as well as of either opponent, and they are obliged to reply.

(49) The player who draws the last card of the stock pile, must discard unless he melds out. Should this discard be playable on the exposed melds of the opponents, the left hand opponent is compelled to take the up-card, meld it on his ex-

posed meld, and take the balance of the up-pile.

This continuance of play after the stock pile is exhausted, is called "forcing". A player who is "forced" must take the up-card and then discard. This discard in turn may be a "forcing" card, that is, a card which is playable on the opponents' exposed meld. This "forces" the next player to take the card. Thus play continues until one of the players discards a card which is not playable by his left hand opponent. During a "force", should the up-card be playable with cards concealed in a hand, the player may take it if he wishes, but he is not compelled to. If he declines to take it, the hand is over. There may be no "force" plays, when the discard pile is frozen.

(50) After the stock is exhausted, a player who holds one card must, if he can, take a one card discard pile and meld out.

(51) If no player melds out, the scores are counted, but neither side receives the going-out bonus.

(52) If the last card of the stock pile is a red three (which cannot be replaced because there are no more cards with which to replace it) the hand is automatically ended and the scores are counted.

### PRIZE PILE

(53) The up-pile becomes a prize pile (that is, it becomes frozen) when it contains a wild card or a red three. Such a pile may be taken only with a concealed natural pair matching the last discard.

(54) At the beginning of the game, if the up card happens to be a red three or a wild card, it is immediately covered with the top card of the stock pile, and the pile remains frozen until someone takes it up.

(55) During the game any player may discard a wild card, thus freezing the pile. After that any player may, as many times as he chooses, discard other wild cards into the up-pile. A wild card so played, is a stop card, in that it may not be picked up by the next player. It will be recalled that three deuces or three Jokers do not constitute a meld.

(56) A frozen discard pile (prize pile) may not be taken even though a subsequent up-card is playable on an exposed meld, unless the player seeking to take the pile also has a matching pair in his hand. (For example: The pile is frozen, East and West have melded 9s, a nine is discarded by South and is presently the up-card; West may not take

the pile unless he has a natural pair of 9s concealed in his hand.)

### RED THREES

(57) The red threes are bonus cards and do not participate in the actual play of a hand. When a player draws a red three from the stock he must place it immediately face up on the table, and replace it by drawing another card from the stock, in order to bring his hand up to the required number of cards.

(a) If a player is dealt any red threes as part of his original hand, he waits until his first turn to play, places them on the table face up before him, replenishes his hand from the stock, and then makes his proper play.

(b) If a player picks up a discard pile containing one or more red threes (they could have gotten there only by having been turned up by the dealer as the up-card), he places them face up on the table, and subsequently receives the prescribed bonus, but he does not draw from the stock to replace them.

(c) If the last card of the stock is a red three, the player who draws it places it face up on the table, melds if he can, but may not discard.

(*d*) If a player fails to replenish his hand for a red three and the error is not discovered until the next player has drawn, play continues without correction.

(*e*) When play ends, a partnership that has melded is credited with 100 points for each of its red threes, or with 800 points for all four red threes. If the partnership has failed to make an initial meld before the conclusion of the hand, then instead of being credited with 100 points for each red three or with 800 points for all four red threes, that sum is deducted from their score.

(*f*) When a player inadvertently fails to place a red three on the table at his first opportunity, he may correct the error without penalty at any subsequent turn to play. If the deal ends before this correction is made, the guilty side is penalized 500 points.

## PERMISSION TO GO OUT

(58) When a player desires to conclude the play of a hand by going out he may, if he chooses, ask his partner the question "May I go out?" The question is asked after the player has drawn from the stock pile, but before he has made a play from his hand.

That is to say, a player must ask the question before melding or before indicating a possible meld.

(*a*) Asking for permission to go out is not mandatory, it is a privilege which a player may exercise at his own option. He may go out without asking, if he so chooses.

(*b*) The partner of the one making the inquiry must reply by simply saying "Yes" or "No" with no qualifying phrase. The reply is binding upon the partnership.

(*c*) A player may ask for permission to go out before drawing, in which case he has the right to take the discard pile (if able to do so) after receiving an answer to his question.

(*d*) If a player should improperly ask permission during the play of cards from his hand, he must go out, regardless of partner's answer.

(*e*) If a player asks his partner for permission to go out, receives the answer "Yes" and then finds that he is not able to go out, his side is penalized 100 points.

(*f*) If a player improperly asks for permission to go out after he has melded or indicated a meld, he MUST go out.

(*g*) If this law is violated by the illicit giving of

information, either opponent may require the player to go out, or prohibit him from going out. This would be the case if a player after asking the question but, before receiving a reply, melds, indicates a meld or in some other way imparts material information to his partner.

## IRREGULARITIES

(59) If a player draws too many cards he must correct the error by discarding without drawing until his hand is correct. If, for example, he draws two cards instead of one, so that after discarding he still holds twelve cards, the next time it comes his turn he does not draw but he does discard in order to bring his hand to the required number. If the player has drawn two extra cards he may not draw for the next two rounds, but he must discard each round.

(60) If a player forgets to draw but does make a discard he may be required to take the top card of the stock if attention is called to his omission before the next player has drawn.

(61) If in making his initial meld a player spreads less than the required count he must make the count sufficient if possible by adding additional cards. If

he is unable to do so there is a penalty of 100 points and he is further required to discard one of the cards which he attempted to meld. He then picks up the remainder and play proceeds normally.[2]

It is argued that if a strict penalty is not enforced the door will be opened to unethical practices by players deliberately exposing cards so that their partners might profit by the information. To this view I do not subscribe. It is never the purpose of rules to prevent cheating. It is the scope of the laws to administer justice. The sound penalty for unethical practices is social ostracism and I am firmly convinced that the Argentines have a much better solution to the problem and that there was no need to change the provisions of the original code in this respect.

According to the New York version the offender must leave his cards exposed on the table and must keep discarding them, one at a time, until he is able to make the requirement for the initial meld. (62) If a player fails to expose a red three at the first proper opportunity, he may correct the error without penalty at any subsequent turn to play. If

[2]The reader's attention is called to the fact that this statement of the law is at variance with the code employed by the Regency Club, but is the original provision contained in the Argentine Code. I favor it because I feel that it is more humane.

the hand ends before he has done this, he is penalized 500 points.

(63) A player who takes the discard pile (regardless of the number of cards it contains) into his hand should be called for it and required to leave it on the table. However, there is no penalty if such player has already shown the cards from his hand that give him the right to take up the discard pile.

If any question arises as to the right to take the pile because of his taking it into his hand prematurely the opponents may require him to replace the discard pile and to draw from the stock pile instead. When it is difficult to determine what cards were picked up from the discard pile the non-offending side becomes the judge of the facts.

(64) If a player makes a meld including more than three wild cards, or attempts to add a wild one to a meld that contains three wild cards (except as provided in law 33), he is required, if able to do so, to correct the error by placing at least one of the wild cards with another meld already on the table or by melding the wild card in any other manner. If he is unable to rectify the error the additional card should be treated as an exposed card.

(65) If a player asks his partner for permission to go out, he must proceed to go out if his partner's

answer is in the affirmative, and opponent may insist upon his going out if he shows or indicates any meld before receiving his partner's answer; or if the form of his question or of his partner's negative reply is designed to convey improper information.

(66) If a player asks for permission to go out and receives it and then discovers that he is unable to go out he must expose his hand, meld what he can and his other cards are exposed and are subject to be discarded at the player's next turn.

(67) There is no penalty for an illegal meld if the next opponent plays in turn before attention is called to it, but in such cases cards improperly exposed on an illegal meld that cannot be rectified must be replaced in the offender's hand.

## POINT PENALTIES

(68) Both the Argentine and American Codes provide for point penalties for certain infractions. It has been my observation that point penalties are not looked upon generally with great favor among players. Some of them, therefore, prefer not to enforce them. By mutual agreement players may decide against the use of point penalties, but where they apply the following is the scale:

| For an illegal draw | 50 points |
|---|---|
| For drawing out of turn (plus an additional 100 points if the offender adds the card improperly drawn to his hand) | 100 points |
| For inability to go out after asking permission and receiving consent | 100 points |
| For melding out of turn | 100 points |

### THE PROPRIETIES

(The proprieties herein outlined are a paraphrase of those established in the code of the American Contract Bridge League)

It is bad sportsmanship to profit by information gained as the result of an irregularity committed by one's own side for which no penalty, or a penalty commensurate with the information gained, is prescribed.

It is highly improper to infringe a law deliberately whether or not a penalty is prescribed.

It is improper to

(a) Indicate, in any way, approval or disapproval of partner's play.

(b) Give by word, manner or gesture an indication of the nature of the hand held.

(c) Make a remark or gesture asking a question from which an inference may be drawn.

(d) Make an unnecessary hesitation or remark which may have the effect of deceiving the opponents.

# VII

## Questions and Answers

**Q.** In making the initial meld must I meld all cards of the same denomination?

**A.** No. You may meld as many different spreads as you choose. For example in order to make up 90 for the initial meld you may meld three Kings, three Jacks and three 10s, though it probably wouldn't be a good idea to do so, nevertheless it is legal.

**Q.** At the end of the hand in counting up the mixed Canasta, can you count the 300 and then also count the individual cards?

**A.** Yes. You have taken the bonus of 300 points for the Canasta, which is considered part of your base score, and then all the cards included in the Canasta are added to your score. The wild cards count: 50 for the Joker, and 20 for the deuce, regardless of what they represent.

Q. If one side needs 120 to meld, and gets a minus
score at the end of a deal, cutting their score from
3100 to 2700, what count is required to meld in
the next deal? 120 or 90?

A. The requirement for the initial meld is now 90
points. The laws clearly indicate that when your
score is 3000 or over the requirement for the
initial meld is 120. When it is between 1500 and
2995, the requirement for the initial meld is 90.
Anyone with a 2700 point score requires 90 for
the initial meld. The requirement applies to your
present score, not to any past score.

Q. Neither side has melded, and after two rounds of
play I spread 120 (this was the requirement for
our initial meld) and then attempted to take up
the discard pile which had a Queen on top, to be
used with one Queen and a deuce. My opponents
refused to permit this. I contend that having
made my initial meld I am now eligible to pick
up the discard pile with one matching card and
a wild card. Who is right?

A. Your opponents were right. On this round you
may not pick up the Queen. Your confusion
arises from the sequence of steps comprised in a
play. They are as follows: 1) The draw; 2) The

meld (optional); 3) The discard. These steps
must be taken in precisely that order. You don't
meld first and then draw. You draw first. At the
time when you are about to draw you are not
eligible to take the discard pile with the aid of a
wild card. You therefore meld your 120 and
await your next turn to draw, when you will be
eligible to use the wild card. You would have
been in position to take up the Queen, if you had
melded your 120 last time, which you could have
done.

Q. Our side has spread three red 3s and we have
melded several spreads, but have not completed
a Canasta, at which point the opponents go out.
They claim that we should be charged with 300
points for possession of red 3s. Are they right?

A. No. The charge for possession of red 3s is made
only when that side fails to make a meld. You
have melded and are, therefore, not subject to
this deduction and you receive credit for 300
points. There are some games in which, by special
agreement between the participants, red 3s are
figured as minus unless the side holding them
scores a Canasta. This is a special ground rule
and is not part of any recognized code. Players,
among themselves, may agree on any variation

that they choose but in the absence of a specific agreement you should abide by the rules of the recognized code.

Q.  The play has developed in such a manner that I am embarrassed for discards. I have melded 6 sevens. May I discard one of those 7s?

A.  No. The rules state specifically that the discards must be made from the concealed hand and not from any exposed meld. This is one of the reasons we recommend violently that a player not reduce his hand to too few cards, for discarding under those conditions is most difficult.

Q.  What is the ruling when a player melds out by disposing of all his cards, and his side has not completed a Canasta?

A.  This question can best be answered by the schoolboy who looked at the giraffe and insisted "there ain't no such animal". A player cannot meld out when his side has not melded a Canasta. He is not permitted to dispose of all his cards any more than he would be permitted to throw them under the table. He must retain at least one. And if he permits his hand to be reduced to one card without having completed a Canasta, he is no doubt guilty of bad management.

Q.  It is nearing the end of the hand and the stock pile is exhausted and the discard pile is frozen. My right hand opponent discards an 8, our side has melded five 8s. It is his contention that I must take up the discard pile under the "forcing" rule. I say I need not take it up. Who is right?

A.  Your opponent is wrong. The forcing principle does not apply when the pack is frozen, for a frozen pack may only be taken with a natural pair. It is not only true that you need not take the 8, but actually you are not permitted to, unless you have a pair of 8s.

Q.  Our side had melded a Canasta of eights. The discard pile was not frozen and my right-hand opponent discarded an eight. I added the eight to my closed Canasta and started to take the discard pile. My opponent claimed that I could not do so, as my Canasta was closed. Will you clear this up?

A.  You were entirely right. There is nothing about a closed Canasta that makes it any different from any other meld. You may add cards to a closed Canasta either from your hand or from the discard pile.

Q.  Both sides needed 120. After several rounds I
melded and discarded a four spot. The next
player (his side had not melded) put down two
sixes and started to take the discard pile. He
claimed that as soon as any one melded no one
else needed the initial count. Was he right?

A.  No. When a player makes the initial meld he re-
leases his own side only from the obligation of
the count. The opponents must still get theirs.

Q.  Does the discard of a black three freeze the discard pile?

A.  No. It stops the next player from taking the pile
at that turn, but once he makes his discard the
black three is covered and forgotten.

Q.  You have stated that when a side is minus on the
score there is no point requirement for initial
meld and they may make their first meld with as
little as 15 points. How does a side become
minus?

A.  It is not a good habit, but it comes about when
your opponents have melded out while you still
have a great many cards in your hand. Remem-

ber you are charged with the point value of all cards left in your hand when the adversaries go out. Then, too, you may be charged with red threes you have spread, if you have never melded. For purposes of illustration permit me to describe a horrible nightmare:—You and your partner have cheerfully spread four red threes. After a few rounds one of your opponents melds out while you hold

Joker-Joker-2-2-2-2-A-K-Q-10-8

Your hand counts 240, for which you are charged. Your partner's hand counts 160, and you are charged with 800 points for the red threes. Your side starts out with a score of minus *1200*. If this ever happens to you the Ripley organization would like to hear about it, and if it's any comfort to you, you may make the initial meld next time, assuming you have survived, with only 15 points.

Q. **Is there any authority for a variation of the game which permits a player to CALL OUT when he passes the 5000 mark during the play of a hand, just as in the game of Casino?**

A. There is no authority whatsoever for any such practice. The laws specifically provide that each deal must be completed.

**Q.** Is a natural Canasta of deuces a legal meld?

**A.** No. Deuces may be named for any natural card, but the 2 does not exist as a natural card. It does in Oklahoma but not in Canasta. Each meld must have at least two natural cards.

**Q.** Can each team have a different requirement for the initial meld? We have scored 1230 points, and the opponents have a score of 3100 points. Does the 120 initial meld apply to us as well as to them?

**A.** No. Each side here has a different requirement for the initial meld. As with race horses, it is weight for age. A 2 year old is not expected to carry as much weight as a 4 year old. The team with the 3100 points requires an initial meld of 120, whereas you, having only 1230, require an initial meld of only 50 points.

**Q.** On the first round of a six-handed game, the third member of our side was able to complete a Canasta and clear his hand. May he go out or must he wait for one round?

**A.** While one must have completed a Canasta before being eligible to go out, the completion of the Canasta may be accomplished in the act of going out, so that your team-mate was eligible to go out on the first round.

Q. Having no Canasta, but one card in my hand, I draw a card which may be melded. May I do so and refrain from discarding?

A. Obviously not. Each play consists of a draw, a meld and a discard. The draw and the discard are obligatory, only the meld is optional. You must, therefore, discard, and consequently are not in a position to meld that card.

Q. Is trading for a wild card permitted in Canasta as it is in Oklahoma? That is, if I have placed a Joker down and called it a King, may I subsequently pick up the Joker and put a King down in its place, using the Joker as I see fit?

A. Definitely not. This is one respect in which Canasta differs from Oklahoma. No trading of wild cards is permitted.

Q. If I have three black 3s in my hand, and the next player throws a three, may I take it up?

A. No. A black three may never be picked up. It is a stop card. Furthermore, 3s may not be melded

except on the play wherein one of the participants is going out.

**Q.** I have completed a Canasta and am down to
one card, I then draw a red three. May I meld
the red three, discard the other card and go out?

**A.** No. Permit me to call attention to a looseness
in terminology. Properly speaking, one does not
*MELD* a red three, one exposes it and receives
a bonus for having "pulled it out of the pie", but
when one draws a red three out of the stock, he
is not presumed to have made a draw (for purposes of play, he drew a blank). He must, therefore, draw again. Now if he draws a card which
is meldable he may meld it, discard his odd card
and go out.

**Q.** It is early in the second deal, and neither side
has melded, we need 90 for our initial meld.
After a couple of rounds my opponent discards
an 8. I have in my hand—Joker-6-6 and 8-8.
I expose my two 8s and the Joker-6-6, reaching
for the discard pile for my meld adds up to 90.
One of my opponents claimed that I must not
go in for the 8s because my initial meld had not
yet been made, that I must first have 90 on the
table before going in. They, therefore, made me
draw from the stock. Were they right?

A.   They were not and you were done an injustice. The up card may be used in conjunction with a concealed natural pair, to help meet the required count for the initial meld.

Q.   **In order to receive credit for a pure Canasta must the seven cards be assembled in one's hand and laid down at once, or may the Canasta be gradually built on the board?**

A.   The Canasta may be built up by degrees. It would be rare, indeed, to be able to spread seven of a kind out of your hand, and it would be most impractical unless you were playing for a concealed hand.

Q.   **When the opponents go out must I deduct all the cards in my hand, even if some of them constitute melds? Do I receive credit for meldable cards?**

A.   Decidedly not. Meldable cards that are not spread upon the table are chargeable to the player holding them. The deduction you wish to make for cards that might have been melded is applicable to Gin Rummy, but not to Canasta.

Q.   **When a player is able to use the top card of the discard pile, it is his privilege to take the entire** pile, but may he, if he chooses, take only the top card?

A.    No. It's take one, take all.

Q.    A player on a side that has not yet made its initial meld has a Canasta of 6s. I have read in several versions of the game that this is eligible as an initial meld because of the value of the Canasta bonus. In other places I have read that this is not a valid initial meld. Which practice is correct?

A.    The latter. This is not a valid meld, unless the player happens to be going out with a concealed hand. During the early days of Canasta in this country the variation to which you refer was suggested as an innovation and was accepted by some players. I actually included it in my first series of published articles. But the practice has not been accepted by any large group of players and it may be considered to be improper.

# VIII

# Quick Check-List for Scoring

NOTE: The first side to reach a total of 5000 points or more wins the game. If both sides reach the 5000 mark in the same deal, the higher total wins. The final deal is always played out, even though it may be apparent midway through the play that one side has reached 5000 points.

### POINT SCORING

|                                             | Points |
|---------------------------------------------|--------|
| Jokers (Regardless of cards represented)    | 50     |
| Deuces (Regardless of cards represented)    | 20     |
| Aces                                        | 20     |
| Kings through eights                        | 10     |
| Sevens through fours                        | 5      |
| Black threes                                | 5      |

### BONUSES

|                                             | Points |
|---------------------------------------------|--------|
| Natural Canasta (No wild cards)             | 500    |
| Mixed Canasta (One or more wild cards)      | 300    |

| | |
|---|---|
| Red three | 100 |
| Four red threes (One partnership) | 800 |
| Melding out | 100 |
| Melding out with "concealed" hand | 200 |

### REQUIREMENTS FOR FIRST MELD

| *Team's score* | *Required initial meld* |
|---|---|
| Minus | 0 |
| 0 to 1495 | 50 |
| 1500 to 2995 | 90 |
| 3000 or more | 120 |

### PENALTIES

*Points*

Drawing Out of Turn

    1. Drawn card not added to player's hand. Replace card. Penalty is   100

    2. Drawn card already added to hand. Replace card. Penalty is   200

Irregular Draw

    1. Taking top card of discard (or entire pile) without first putting down matching cards   50

    2. Taking top card of discard without being able to meld   50

*Points*

3. Drawing from stock and seeing or
   exposing another card of the stock    50

Melding Out of Turn    100

Inability to Go Out After Asking Permission and Receiving Consent    100

# CANASTA SCORE PAD

(Tear out or keep as a permanent record)

| | WE | THEY | WE | THEY |
|---|---|---|---|---|
| NAME | | | | |
| Basic | | | | |
| Meld | | | | |
| **Total** | | | | |
| Basic | | | | |
| Meld | | | | |
| **Total** | | | | |
| Basic | | | | |
| Meld | | | | |
| **Total** | | | | |
| Basic | | | | |
| Meld | | | | |
| **Total** | | | | |
| Basic | | | | |
| Meld | | | | |
| **Total** | | | | |
| Basic | | | | |
| Meld | | | | |
| **Total** | | | | |

# CANASTA SCORE PAD

*(Tear out or keep as a permanent record)*

| | WE | THEY | WE | THEY |
|---|---|---|---|---|
| NAME | | | | |
| Basic | | | | |
| Meld | | | | |
| **Total** | | | | |
| Basic | | | | |
| Meld | | | | |
| **Total** | | | | |
| Basic | | | | |
| Meld | | | | |
| **Total** | | | | |
| Basic | | | | |
| Meld | | | | |
| **Total** | | | | |
| Basic | | | | |
| Meld | | | | |
| **Total** | | | | |
| Basic | | | | |
| Meld | | | | |
| **Total** | | | | |

# CANASTA SCORE PAD

*(Tear out or keep as a permanent record)*

|  | WE | THEY | WE | THEY |
|---|---|---|---|---|
| NAME |  |  |  |  |
| Basic |  |  |  |  |
| Meld |  |  |  |  |
| **Total** |  |  |  |  |
| Basic |  |  |  |  |
| Meld |  |  |  |  |
| **Total** |  |  |  |  |
| Basic |  |  |  |  |
| Meld |  |  |  |  |
| **Total** |  |  |  |  |
| Basic |  |  |  |  |
| Meld |  |  |  |  |
| **Total** |  |  |  |  |
| Basic |  |  |  |  |
| Meld |  |  |  |  |
| **Total** |  |  |  |  |
| Basic |  |  |  |  |
| Meld |  |  |  |  |
| **Total** |  |  |  |  |

# CANASTA SCORE PAD

*(Tear out or keep as a permanent record)*

|  | WE | THEY | WE | THEY |
|---|---|---|---|---|
| NAME |  |  |  |  |
| Basic |  |  |  |  |
| Meld |  |  |  |  |
| **Total** |  |  |  |  |
| Basic |  |  |  |  |
| Meld |  |  |  |  |
| **Total** |  |  |  |  |
| Basic |  |  |  |  |
| Meld |  |  |  |  |
| **Total** |  |  |  |  |
| Basic |  |  |  |  |
| Meld |  |  |  |  |
| **Total** |  |  |  |  |
| Basic |  |  |  |  |
| Meld |  |  |  |  |
| **Total** |  |  |  |  |
| Basic |  |  |  |  |
| Meld |  |  |  |  |
| **Total** |  |  |  |  |

# CANASTA SCORE PAD
*(Tear out or keep as a permanent record)*

|        | WE | THEY | WE | THEY |
|--------|----|------|----|------|
| NAME   |    |      |    |      |
| Basic  |    |      |    |      |
| Meld   |    |      |    |      |
| **Total** |    |      |    |      |
| Basic  |    |      |    |      |
| Meld   |    |      |    |      |
| **Total** |    |      |    |      |
| Basic  |    |      |    |      |
| Meld   |    |      |    |      |
| **Total** |    |      |    |      |
| Basic  |    |      |    |      |
| Meld   |    |      |    |      |
| **Total** |    |      |    |      |
| Basic  |    |      |    |      |
| Meld   |    |      |    |      |
| **Total** |    |      |    |      |
| Basic  |    |      |    |      |
| Meld   |    |      |    |      |
| **Total** |    |      |    |      |

# CANASTA SCORE PAD

*(Tear out or keep as a permanent record)*

|       | WE | THEY | WE | THEY |
|-------|----|------|----|------|
| NAME  |    |      |    |      |
| Basic |    |      |    |      |
| Meld  |    |      |    |      |
| **Total** |    |      |    |      |
| Basic |    |      |    |      |
| Meld  |    |      |    |      |
| **Total** |    |      |    |      |
| Basic |    |      |    |      |
| Meld  |    |      |    |      |
| **Total** |    |      |    |      |
| Basic |    |      |    |      |
| Meld  |    |      |    |      |
| **Total** |    |      |    |      |
| Basic |    |      |    |      |
| Meld  |    |      |    |      |
| **Total** |    |      |    |      |
| Basic |    |      |    |      |
| Meld  |    |      |    |      |
| **Total** |    |      |    |      |

# CANASTA SCORE PAD

*(Tear out or keep as a permanent record)*

|  | WE | THEY | WE | THEY |
|---|---|---|---|---|
| NAME |  |  |  |  |
| Basic |  |  |  |  |
| Meld |  |  |  |  |
| **Total** |  |  |  |  |
| Basic |  |  |  |  |
| Meld |  |  |  |  |
| **Total** |  |  |  |  |
| Basic |  |  |  |  |
| Meld |  |  |  |  |
| **Total** |  |  |  |  |
| Basic |  |  |  |  |
| Meld |  |  |  |  |
| **Total** |  |  |  |  |
| Basic |  |  |  |  |
| Meld |  |  |  |  |
| **Total** |  |  |  |  |
| Basic |  |  |  |  |
| Meld |  |  |  |  |
| **Total** |  |  |  |  |

# CANASTA SCORE PAD

*(Tear out or keep as a permanent record)*

|       | WE | THEY | WE | THEY |
|-------|----|------|----|------|
| NAME  |    |      |    |      |
| Basic |    |      |    |      |
| Meld  |    |      |    |      |
| **Total** |    |      |    |      |
| Basic |    |      |    |      |
| Meld  |    |      |    |      |
| **Total** |    |      |    |      |
| Basic |    |      |    |      |
| Meld  |    |      |    |      |
| **Total** |    |      |    |      |
| Basic |    |      |    |      |
| Meld  |    |      |    |      |
| **Total** |    |      |    |      |
| Basic |    |      |    |      |
| Meld  |    |      |    |      |
| **Total** |    |      |    |      |
| Basic |    |      |    |      |
| Meld  |    |      |    |      |
| **Total** |    |      |    |      |

# CANASTA SCORE PAD

*(Tear out or keep as a permanent record)*

| | WE | THEY | WE | THEY |
|---|---|---|---|---|
| NAME | | | | |
| Basic | | | | |
| Meld | | | | |
| **Total** | | | | |
| Basic | | | | |
| Meld | | | | |
| **Total** | | | | |
| Basic | | | | |
| Meld | | | | |
| **Total** | | | | |
| Basic | | | | |
| Meld | | | | |
| **Total** | | | | |
| Basic | | | | |
| Meld | | | | |
| **Total** | | | | |
| Basic | | | | |
| Meld | | | | |
| **Total** | | | | |

# CANASTA SCORE PAD
*(Tear out or keep as a permanent record)*

|  | WE | THEY | WE | THEY |
|---|---|---|---|---|
| NAME |  |  |  |  |
| Basic |  |  |  |  |
| Meld |  |  |  |  |
| **Total** |  |  |  |  |
| Basic |  |  |  |  |
| Meld |  |  |  |  |
| **Total** |  |  |  |  |
| Basic |  |  |  |  |
| Meld |  |  |  |  |
| **Total** |  |  |  |  |
| Basic |  |  |  |  |
| Meld |  |  |  |  |
| **Total** |  |  |  |  |
| Basic |  |  |  |  |
| Meld |  |  |  |  |
| **Total** |  |  |  |  |
| Basic |  |  |  |  |
| Meld |  |  |  |  |
| **Total** |  |  |  |  |

# CANASTA SCORE PAD

*(Tear out or keep as a permanent record)*

| | WE | THEY | WE | THEY |
|---|---|---|---|---|
| NAME | | | | |
| Basic | | | | |
| Meld | | | | |
| **Total** | | | | |
| Basic | | | | |
| Meld | | | | |
| **Total** | | | | |
| Basic | | | | |
| Meld | | | | |
| **Total** | | | | |
| Basic | | | | |
| Meld | | | | |
| **Total** | | | | |
| Basic | | | | |
| Meld | | | | |
| **Total** | | | | |
| Basic | | | | |
| Meld | | | | |
| **Total** | | | | |

# CANASTA SCORE PAD

*(Tear out or keep as a permanent record)*

|  | WE | THEY | WE | THEY |
|---|---|---|---|---|
| NAME |  |  |  |  |
| Basic |  |  |  |  |
| Meld |  |  |  |  |
| **Total** |  |  |  |  |
| Basic |  |  |  |  |
| Meld |  |  |  |  |
| **Total** |  |  |  |  |
| Basic |  |  |  |  |
| Meld |  |  |  |  |
| **Total** |  |  |  |  |
| Basic |  |  |  |  |
| Meld |  |  |  |  |
| **Total** |  |  |  |  |
| Basic |  |  |  |  |
| Meld |  |  |  |  |
| **Total** |  |  |  |  |
| Basic |  |  |  |  |
| Meld |  |  |  |  |
| **Total** |  |  |  |  |

# CANASTA SCORE PAD

*(Tear out or keep as a permanent record)*

|  | WE | THEY | WE | THEY |
|---|---|---|---|---|
| NAME |  |  |  |  |
| Basic |  |  |  |  |
| Meld |  |  |  |  |
| **Total** |  |  |  |  |
| Basic |  |  |  |  |
| Meld |  |  |  |  |
| **Total** |  |  |  |  |
| Basic |  |  |  |  |
| Meld |  |  |  |  |
| **Total** |  |  |  |  |
| Basic |  |  |  |  |
| Meld |  |  |  |  |
| **Total** |  |  |  |  |
| Basic |  |  |  |  |
| Meld |  |  |  |  |
| **Total** |  |  |  |  |
| Basic |  |  |  |  |
| Meld |  |  |  |  |
| **Total** |  |  |  |  |

# CANASTA SCORE PAD

*(Tear out or keep as a permanent record)*

| | WE | THEY | WE | THEY |
|---|---|---|---|---|
| NAME | | | | |
| Basic | | | | |
| Meld | | | | |
| **Total** | | | | |
| Basic | | | | |
| Meld | | | | |
| **Total** | | | | |
| Basic | | | | |
| Meld | | | | |
| **Total** | | | | |
| Basic | | | | |
| Meld | | | | |
| **Total** | | | | |
| Basic | | | | |
| Meld | | | | |
| **Total** | | | | |
| Basic | | | | |
| Meld | | | | |
| **Total** | | | | |

# CANASTA SCORE PAD
*(Tear out or keep as a permanent record)*

| | WE | THEY | WE | THEY |
|---|---|---|---|---|
| NAME | | | | |
| Basic | | | | |
| Meld | | | | |
| **Total** | | | | |
| Basic | | | | |
| Meld | | | | |
| **Total** | | | | |
| Basic | | | | |
| Meld | | | | |
| **Total** | | | | |
| Basic | | | | |
| Meld | | | | |
| **Total** | | | | |
| Basic | | | | |
| Meld | | | | |
| **Total** | | | | |
| Basic | | | | |
| Meld | | | | |
| **Total** | | | | |

# CANASTA SCORE PAD
*(Tear out or keep as a permanent record)*

|  | WE | THEY | WE | THEY |
|---|---|---|---|---|
| NAME |  |  |  |  |
| Basic |  |  |  |  |
| Meld |  |  |  |  |
| **Total** |  |  |  |  |
| Basic |  |  |  |  |
| Meld |  |  |  |  |
| **Total** |  |  |  |  |
| Basic |  |  |  |  |
| Meld |  |  |  |  |
| **Total** |  |  |  |  |
| Basic |  |  |  |  |
| Meld |  |  |  |  |
| **Total** |  |  |  |  |
| Basic |  |  |  |  |
| Meld |  |  |  |  |
| **Total** |  |  |  |  |
| Basic |  |  |  |  |
| Meld |  |  |  |  |
| **Total** |  |  |  |  |

# CANASTA SCORE PAD
*(Tear out or keep as a permanent record)*

| | WE | THEY | WE | THEY |
|---|---|---|---|---|
| **NAME** | | | | |
| Basic | | | | |
| Meld | | | | |
| **Total** | | | | |
| Basic | | | | |
| Meld | | | | |
| **Total** | | | | |
| Basic | | | | |
| Meld | | | | |
| **Total** | | | | |
| Basic | | | | |
| Meld | | | | |
| **Total** | | | | |
| Basic | | | | |
| Meld | | | | |
| **Total** | | | | |
| Basic | | | | |
| Meld | | | | |
| **Total** | | | | |

# CANASTA SCORE PAD
*(Tear out or keep as a permanent record)*

|  | WE | THEY | WE | THEY |
|---|---|---|---|---|
| NAME |  |  |  |  |
| Basic |  |  |  |  |
| Meld |  |  |  |  |
| **Total** |  |  |  |  |
| Basic |  |  |  |  |
| Meld |  |  |  |  |
| **Total** |  |  |  |  |
| Basic |  |  |  |  |
| Meld |  |  |  |  |
| **Total** |  |  |  |  |
| Basic |  |  |  |  |
| Meld |  |  |  |  |
| **Total** |  |  |  |  |
| Basic |  |  |  |  |
| Meld |  |  |  |  |
| **Total** |  |  |  |  |
| Basic |  |  |  |  |
| Meld |  |  |  |  |
| **Total** |  |  |  |  |

# CANASTA SCORE PAD

*(Tear out or keep as a permanent record)*

|  | WE | THEY | WE | THEY |
|---|---|---|---|---|
| NAME |  |  |  |  |
| Basic |  |  |  |  |
| Meld |  |  |  |  |
| **Total** |  |  |  |  |
| Basic |  |  |  |  |
| Meld |  |  |  |  |
| **Total** |  |  |  |  |
| Basic |  |  |  |  |
| Meld |  |  |  |  |
| **Total** |  |  |  |  |
| Basic |  |  |  |  |
| Meld |  |  |  |  |
| **Total** |  |  |  |  |
| Basic |  |  |  |  |
| Meld |  |  |  |  |
| **Total** |  |  |  |  |
| Basic |  |  |  |  |
| Meld |  |  |  |  |
| **Total** |  |  |  |  |

# CANASTA SCORE PAD
*(Tear out or keep as a permanent record)*

| NAME | WE | THEY | WE | THEY |
|---|---|---|---|---|
| Basic | | | | |
| Meld | | | | |
| **Total** | | | | |
| Basic | | | | |
| Meld | | | | |
| **Total** | | | | |
| Basic | | | | |
| Meld | | | | |
| **Total** | | | | |
| Basic | | | | |
| Meld | | | | |
| **Total** | | | | |
| Basic | | | | |
| Meld | | | | |
| **Total** | | | | |
| Basic | | | | |
| Meld | | | | |
| **Total** | | | | |

# CANASTA SCORE PAD

*(Tear out or keep as a permanent record)*

|        | WE | THEY | WE | THEY |
|--------|----|------|----|------|
| NAME   |    |      |    |      |
| Basic  |    |      |    |      |
| Meld   |    |      |    |      |
| **Total** |    |      |    |      |
| Basic  |    |      |    |      |
| Meld   |    |      |    |      |
| **Total** |    |      |    |      |
| Basic  |    |      |    |      |
| Meld   |    |      |    |      |
| **Total** |    |      |    |      |
| Basic  |    |      |    |      |
| Meld   |    |      |    |      |
| **Total** |    |      |    |      |
| Basic  |    |      |    |      |
| Meld   |    |      |    |      |
| **Total** |    |      |    |      |
| Basic  |    |      |    |      |
| Meld   |    |      |    |      |
| **Total** |    |      |    |      |

# CANASTA SCORE PAD

*(Tear out or keep as a permanent record)*

|        | WE | THEY | WE | THEY |
|--------|----|------|----|------|
| NAME   |    |      |    |      |
| Basic  |    |      |    |      |
| Meld   |    |      |    |      |
| **Total** |  |      |    |      |
| Basic  |    |      |    |      |
| Meld   |    |      |    |      |
| **Total** |  |      |    |      |
| Basic  |    |      |    |      |
| Meld   |    |      |    |      |
| **Total** |  |      |    |      |
| Basic  |    |      |    |      |
| Meld   |    |      |    |      |
| **Total** |  |      |    |      |
| Basic  |    |      |    |      |
| Meld   |    |      |    |      |
| **Total** |  |      |    |      |
| Basic  |    |      |    |      |
| Meld   |    |      |    |      |
| **Total** |  |      |    |      |

# Which of these popular new Permabooks do you want?

---

*New titles are added monthly. See your local dealer for these and other new Permabooks. If your dealer is unable to supply certain titles, send 35¢ for each book (plus 5¢ per book for postage and handling) to*

PERMABOOKS
Mail Order Department
Garden City, New York